Women of Courage

by
Susan Yeandle

Editorial Consultant, Sheila Pantry

100 YEARS OF
1893
WOMEN
1993
FACTORY INSPECTORS

London: HMSO

Contents

100 YEARS OF
WOMEN
1893
1993
FACTORY INSPECTORS

Foreword

Women of Courage shows how inspectors secure acceptable standards of health and safety in the workplace often against the odds.

As Chief Inspector of Factories, it is my pleasure to acknowledge the contributions made by women inspectors over the past 100 years. I hope *Women of Courage* will encourage others to join the Inspectorate part of the Health and Safety Executive, and help us achieve our goal of safe and healthy working conditions for all in the twenty-first century.

David Eves

Chief Inspector of Factories

Acknowledgements

The author and editorial consultant are most grateful for the assistance of many people in assembling the material for the book. Without these contributions the book could not have been written.

Anita Bufton gave valuable research assistance in selecting material from HSE's Information Services historical collection, and Miss Norah Curry, retired inspector, made numerous helpful contributions from her own investigations, as well as giving a generous interview. Sincere thanks also to other former and current women inspectors who gave interviews, supplied various memorabilia and completed questionnaires: Miss Vera Chinn, Miss Cecily Tabb, Dr Marianne Woolgar, and others still in post who remain anonymous. Other information was supplied by: Mr Dick Gates, Miss Beryl Leighton, Mr Jim Hammer, Mr Eric Purcell, Miss Veronica Roach, Mr Cyril Burgess, Mrs Jennifer Clark, University of Loughborough Archivist, the photographic team of HSE's Research and Laboratory Services Division; Wendy Howe and Grahame Caine of HSE's Publications Section.

Introduction

Women of Courage identifies the changing and challenging role of lady inspectors, as they were first called, over the last 100 years. The first two were appointed on 5 May 1893. This book celebrates the centenary of these appointments, and acknowledges the contribution made by women inspectors. It marks the important impact women have made on health and safety at work in the United Kingdom, and in some cases further afield. Particularly notable were the achievements of women inspectors and women workers more generally during the two world wars.

The illustrations give a dramatic indication of how much workplaces where women were employed have improved over the period. This has been especially noticeable during the preparation of the book in 1992, the year of European Safety, Hygiene and Health Protection at Work, when much new legislation is coming into force across Europe which will further improve working conditions.

The photographs and other illustrations are drawn from the extensive and expanding 'historical collection' which has been assembled over the past 15 years by the Health and Safety Executive Information Services. This unique collection is protected by the Public Records Act, and all items within it are indexed in HSELINE, HSE's publicly available database.

The narrative, by Dr Sue Yeandle, Senior Lecturer in the School of Health and Community Studies at Sheffield Hallam University, is the result of research in HSE's historical collection and original research including interviews with retired women inspectors. In addition, much correspondence on this subject has been accumulated by Sheila Pantry, HSE's Head of Information Services and Editorial Consultant. This material has been added to the historical collection.

Women enter the Factory Inspectorate

"In no government work

were women more successful

than as factory inspectors

under the Home Office."

(Holcombe 1973, p170)

This verdict of the historian Lee Holcombe is reflected in numerous other tributes to the work of the early 'Lady Inspectors', made both by their contemporaries and by subsequent commentators. Their own accounts, describing their activities in extraordinary detail in the annual reports of the Chief Inspector of Factories and elsewhere, bear witness to their enthusiasm, dedication, expertise and sheer hard work.

The idea that women might have a role to play in the work of factory inspection was not one which found immediate favour when it was first mooted in the last quarter of the 19th century. The Factory Inspectorate was by this time a well-established and respected arm of government, and the achievements of factory inspectors over 50 years were especially obvious to those with a close interest in the welfare of the labouring classes: middle class reformers and politicians of philanthropic intent, and workers' representatives and trades unionists. Factory inspectors had been enforcing the factory legislation since 1833, and were widely regarded as having been responsible for significant improvements in the welfare of child workers.

The way forward for those with a special interest in women's welfare and rights, however, was not immediately clear. Some held the view that the protective legislation of the mid-19th century had done little genuinely to improve women's situation: some feared that any extension of protective legislation would lead to women's greater unemployment and hardship.

Early influences: Emma Paterson

Emma Paterson, the founder in 1874 of the Women's Protective and Provident League (WPPL), was the daughter of a headmaster, but a woman with extensive contact with working people, through her own apprenticeship as a bookbinder and through her work as Secretary to the Working Men's Club and Institute Union. In the United States in the early 1870s she became interested in women's trade union representation and, returning to Britain, founded the WPPL which aimed to encourage the establishment, in every trade where women were employed, of a protective and benefit union (Boston, p30).

In 1878, Paterson advocated the appointment of women as inspectors of factories when she addressed the Bristol TUC, and was successful in getting a resolution to this effect passed (Martindale, 1938 p51). The following year, at the main Trades Union Congress of 1879, she spoke in favour of the appointment of working class women as factory inspectors. The need to draw more inspectors from the ranks of working people had become a regular demand emanating from the TUC. Paterson was specific about the

kind of women she believed it was necessary to appoint, and the 1879 TUC Annual Report records that 'workwomen' had called for the appointment of 'women - not ladies, but practical working women' as factory inspectors (Jones, 1988).

Despite support from other women representatives over subsequent years, the TUC did not take up this demand on any serious scale with government. The Chief Inspector of Factories chose this moment to observe in his annual report of 1879 :

❝ I doubt very much whether the office of factory inspector is one suitable for women. ... The general and multifarious duties of an inspector of factories would really be incompatible with the gentle and home-loving character of a woman. ... Factory inspecting requires activity and acumen and the stern authority of a man to enforce obedience to his interrogatories. It is not an agreeable duty for a man, but I cannot conceive that such functions would commend themselves to a woman, or that she could successfully discharge them. I question the success of a female inspector in appearing at a metropolitan police court,

Miss Mary Paterson CBE, appointed one of the first two
Lady Inspectors, 8 May 1893

Miss May Abraham, appointed one of the first two Lady Inspectors, 6 May 1893

conducting her case and having to submit herself to the cross-examination of an astute attorney. ... It has been argued that where women are employed some enquiries could be more appropriately made by women ... but it is seldom necessary to put a single question to a female. " (Alexander Redgrave, quoted in Martindale, 1938 p51-2).

With no encouragement in this quarter, it fell, therefore, to Emma Paterson to lead a campaign for women's entry into the Factory Inspectorate: this she did by building on support in various quarters, and by organising a conference in 1881 presided over by Lord Shaftesbury. There began a shift in public opinion about the matter, and it was taken up on several occasions in Parliament. In 1890, a large meeting on the topic was organised at the Old Assembly Hall in the Mile End Road, supported by the London Trade Unions and many trades councils throughout the country (Jones, 1988). That same year, the London Women's Trades Council tried unsuccessfully to take a deputation to the Home Office, although it did gain the chance of explaining in detail why women were needed as inspectors. Even as late as 1892, one year before the first appointments, the Home Secretary was only making the most cautious of replies to questions asking for the appointment of women inspectors. 'It might', he answered, and as Martindale records, 'be tried as an experiment' (p53).

The Royal Commission on Labour

Yet the views of Chief Inspector Redgrave were increasingly at variance with the times. The 1890s saw a variety of changes in the position of women, and a developing acceptance of a more prominent public role for women. It was also a decade of greater state intervention in the lives of working people. Not least among the developments of this decade were the deliberations of the Royal Commission on Labour, which began work in 1891 and reported in 1894.

The significance of this Commission so far as women factory inspectors were concerned cannot be over-estimated: May Abraham and Mary Paterson, the two women appointed as the first Lady Inspectors in 1893, had both been closely involved with it (Miss Abraham as one of the four Lady Assistant Commissioners, and Miss Paterson as clerk and precis writer). Two of the other early Lady Inspectors, Adelaide Anderson and Anna Tracey, had also been clerks to the Commission (Harrison, 1990 p80).

Redgrave maintained his opposition to women inspectors, but his retirement in 1891 removed one of the obstacles to their appointment. The work of the Lady Assistant Commissioners served to smooth the path in other ways: their reports for the Royal Commission on Labour on the conditions of employed women revealed the many aspects of industrial employment which were undermining women's health and family lives, and the quality of the Lady Commissioners' work showed how effective women could be in the service of the state.

Lady Dilke

May Abraham had gained her position as a Lady Assistant Commissioner on the Royal Commission on Labour through her connection with Lady Dilke, to whom she was secretary, and who had effectively taken the place of Emma Paterson at the helm of the Women's Protective and Provident League on her death in 1886. Lady Dilke was responsible for implementing a variety of changes in the policies of the League, and for its change of name in the early 1890s to the Women's Trade Union League (Boston, 1980 p35).

The policy changes were important, for the League now ceased resisting legislation restricting women's working hours, and began to campaign for extension of the protective legislation for women.

May Abraham had come to London in 1888 from her native Dublin, following the death of her father. She had little but her letter of introduction to Emilia Lady Dilke, who was already deeply involved in social questions and especially the rights of working women. Lady Dilke was also well connected through her marriage to the Liberal MP Sir Charles Dilke.

Asquith

After the General Election of August 1892 the Liberals came to power led by William Gladstone. Dilke was re-elected an MP, and H H Asquith was appointed Home Secretary. Asquith was held in high regard by Dilke, had taken a keen interest in the deliberations of the Royal Commission on Labour (and thus was aware that numerous witnesses had supported the appointment of women factory inspectors), and was keen to give special attention to industrial affairs in his new post.

on or before the 7⁺ September next.

I am, Sir,

Your obedient Servant

Alfeyenovann

P.S. If you find in any case that either of the Lady Inspectors viz. Miss Abraham or Miss Paterson has already made enquiries, omit that place from your list.

Inspector of factories circular, 1893

He was lobbied extensively about women inspectors, by the Women's Liberal Federation (led by Lady Aberdeen), by the Scottish Liberal Association, by the Society for Promoting the Employment of Women, and by the Women's Trade Union Association. All put the case for women inspectors (McFeely, 1988 p13-14).

Despite continuing opposition from within the Factory Inspectorate, which had been reduced to making comments about women's dress in support of its position - 'unless Female Inspectors wore garments properly arranged, as those of the operatives are, they would run a great danger to which men Inspectors are not liable' (unsigned Home Office memorandum, July 1891, quoted by McFeely) - Asquith made the following announcement when he spoke to the National Liberal Federation in January 1893:

66 I hope I may be able at the same time to do something - it will not be much - to gratify the desire of our lady friends for female inspection.99 (quoted in Martindale, 1938 p53)

First appointments

The time, then, had come for the appointment of the first women factory inspectors. Martindale, who was appointed in 1902 and was herself a prominent inspector in later years, is surely right to comment:

66 Mr Asquith was far from correct when he said 'it will not be much'. He appointed two women who brought to their work a high standard and great devotion, and he gave them a liberal starting-point and a wide field of activity. He realized that, when opening a new career to women, the future would depend on the choice of the first women to fill the posts, and he chose well. Indeed, he had done something to establish what proved, as the years went on, to be one of the greatest public services rendered by women.99 (Martindale, 1938 p53-4).

Boston has commented more recently that:

66 The appointment of women to the Factory Inspectorate marked a great advance for women. For the first time the government had given women highly responsible jobs. Their appointment was remarkable since their work involved travelling extensively around the British Isles, not just to factories, but to back-street workshops and to places like the wilds of Donegal. They were required to have an intimate knowledge of the law regarding factory legislation and the Truck Acts and, what was more, they had to be able to argue their case in court thirty years before women were officially admitted to the bar. 99 (Boston, 1980 p36-7)

Not all that women workers and their representatives had been calling for had been achieved. Jones (1988) has observed that the women appointed were not the practical working women Emma Paterson spoke of when she began campaigning for women inspectors in the 1870s. The appointments were of educated ladies from the middle class, and they opened up for such women a new career field in the public service. The class differences between the early women inspectors and the women whose trades they inspected were indeed great: their achievements on behalf of women workers are I think not diminished by recognition of this fact, or of their quite openly moral position on some of the labour questions of the day.

May Abraham and Mary Paterson began work as Lady Inspectors in May 1893. They were appointed to perform their duties in peripatetic fashion, and were based in London at the Home Office and in Glasgow respectively. They were appointed at an annual salary of £200 (as compared with the male inspectors' pay at that time of £300-320), and were expected to travel widely and to conduct their investigations independently. The Chief Inspector of Factories reports in 1893 that during the year they travelled 3464 and 4270 miles respectively, and claimed expenses of £65.0s.4d and £41.9s 1d. Her Majesty's Chief Inspector of Factories, R E Sprague Oram, commented in his report to the Home Secretary:

> 66 Being of the opinion that the field for the employment of women, within the limits of their own special capacities and aptitudes, should be as wide and as large as you could possibly make it, and that there is no field in which they could more usefully or fruitfully be employed than in looking after the health and the industrial conditions under which their fellow women labour in the factories and workshops, you appointed two ladies as inspectors whose labour have already been found most useful: the appointment of two others, with suitable qualifications, which has been determined upon, will, I believe, also be a great additional advantage to the department. 99 (ARCI, 1893 p10)

Miss Abraham and Miss Paterson had indeed been extremely busy in their work almost from the moment of appointment. Miss Abraham had made inspections in millinery, dressmaking and tailoring workshops in London and had visited 11 towns in the course of her enquiries into the laundry and lucifer match trades. Her work had included investigation of overtime, ventilation, overcrowding, fire escapes, accidents and the Truck Acts. She had already been appointed a member of the Departmental Committee on lucifer match manufacture, and was to be influential in designating this as one of the 'dangerous trades'.

Abraham and Paterson were fortunate in Oram as their Chief Inspector. He was keen that they should work independently and not become absorbed into the general work of the Inspectorate. He saw to it that they reported directly to him, and took trouble to praise their work in his annual reports. Mr Gould, Superintending Inspector in Scotland, is quoted 'I may speak most highly of her (Miss Paterson's) work, which appears to be thorough and efficiently performed' (ARCI, 1893). Oram himself also expressed enthusiasm for their work in less public places. In a memorandum to Sir Godfrey Lushington, the Under Secretary at the Home Office, he stated:

> 66 I think it desirable that they should continue to occupy a position entirely independent of H M Inspectors and that they should be peripatetic, to go wherever their services are required, forwarding their reports to the Chief Inspector and receiving instructions from him. 99 (McFeely, 1988 p20-1)

Following on the success of these first appointments, two further educated women were appointed in early 1894: Lucy Deane and Adelaide Anderson. Miss Deane had gone to considerable lengths to prepare herself for this appointment, and had taken great trouble to make herself and her abilities known to those who could influence her appointment. She had experience as a sanitary inspector and public health lecturer and had first met May Abraham in November 1893. By January 1894 she had taken tea

Miss Adelaide Anderson, appointed early 1894 following the success of the first appointments

with Emilia Lady Dilke, had an interview with Asquith's private secretary, H J Tennant, and spoken with Alexander Redgrave, the retired Chief Inspector, whom she described in her diary as 'a kindly old man' despite his open disapproval of the appointment of women as inspectors (McFeely p22-3).

Miss Anderson, who was a niece of Elizabeth Garrett Anderson, had studied moral science at Girton College, Cambridge, and had worked on the Royal Commission on Labour. She and Deane sat the civil service examination together at 10 o'clock on 30 March 1894. McFeely, who studied Deane's diaries, records:

" 'I was seized with exam fright' Lucy Deane wrote on 30 March, but though she suspected her performance on the arithmetic paper was 'shameful' she felt more confident about composition and the section on the Factory Acts. At 6.15, having had only one 20-minute break she came home 'dead beat and very nervous'. The next day she returned for an hour-long oral test on the Factory Acts; she thought she had performed well. And indeed she passed the examination. Anderson, however, had to retake one section, which she had failed, before she could be accepted. " (1988 p25-6)

Meanwhile, Oram was both ensuring that the Lady Inspectors could work without undue interference with the activities of the male inspectors and thinking about the future organisation of the Lady Inspectors' work. His memoranda indicate that he was firmly committed to the separate organisation and conduct of the Lady Inspectors' work.

In 1894 this was made clear in his annual report:

" The (Lady) Inspectors receive and attend to any complaint received from or relating to the employment of women in any part of the UK. It is advisable that they should form a separate and distinct department if they are to be permanently useful. " (ARCI, 1894 p11)

A fifth Lady Inspector, Rose Squire, was added to this small group in January 1896. She, too, recorded her thoughts about her appointment, and later published them, noting 'I was the only candidate at the Civil Service Examination, which was held by the Commissioners for me alone.' (Squire, 1927 p31-2)

Miss Squire was to become a prominent inspector and civil servant, and the reports of the Chief Inspector for those early years are full of her observations and activities. She had known Lucy Deane in her previous work as a sanitary inspector, and was brought to the attention of the Home Secretary, whose recommendation was required for all appointments to the Factory Inspectorate at that time, as a result of this connection.

The Women's Branch

The four Lady Inspectors based in London (Mary Paterson remained in Scotland) were in a position to meet frequently and to consider how they might consolidate and protect their position within the Inspectorate. They felt the need to do this because of the inherent precariousness of the support of their Home Secretary, Asquith, and because of the impending retirement of Oram, who had been at the Department since 1861.

Squire recalls with some retrospective amazement the conditions under which they worked in those early years:

66 It now seems strange to recall that no office room was assigned to us until some time later, the Chief Inspector gave us verbal instructions and looked after us with a fatherly interest ..... then, and for a long time to come, all official correspondence was written by hand; if copies were required copying ink and a hand press were used - we had no clerks and there was no typing; the telephone, if in use at all, was a luxury for highest officials only. 99 (Squire, 1927 p32)

They determined, without consultation with Mary Paterson in Glasgow, it seems, to request that one of their number be appointed to take charge of the Lady Inspectors' work: this would effectively create a Women's Branch, and considerably strengthen their position. Oram, ever their advocate, favoured the idea, and May Abraham was selected, it seems under protest, but succumbing to Lucy Deane's powers of persuasion, to occupy the more senior position.

The appointment was announced by Sir Matthew White Ridley, the new Conservative Home Secretary under Lord Salisbury's premiership, at the same time as that of the new Chief Inspector of Factories: Oram was succeeded by an appointee from outside the Inspectorate, Dr Arthur Whitelegge. Deane recorded in her diary:

66 The men inspectors furious! at both plans

which come upon them as a sudden shock 99 (19 March 1896, quoted in McFeely, 1988 p46)

Deane and Abraham, alerted to the men inspectors' opposition to the new arrangements:

66 drove to Mr Oram's house and had conference with him ... he at once went straight to Mr Digby (the permanent undersecretary) at HO about it. 99 (ibid)

Fortunately for the Lady Inspectors, Ridley chose to stick to his decision, and the men's protests faded away. May Abraham was now promoted to superintending inspector, a position she occupied until her retirement from the service in May 1897 following her marriage to H J Tennant. It is interesting to note that while Rose Squire records this as her retirement 'on marriage' (Squire, 1937), Adelaide Anderson, who succeeded her, indicates that she retained her position for some time afterwards:

66 Miss Abraham retired from the Inspectorate in May 1897, a year after marriage, and the branch continued from that year until August 1921 under (my) direction. 99 (Anderson, 1922, p13-4)

Certainly May Edith Tennant, Her Majesty's Superintending Inspector of Factories, is listed as a member of the Home Office Dangerous Trades Committee in 1897, and she apparently met Deane in April 1897 while 'preparing to retire at the end of May since her baby was due in July' (McFeely, 1988 p66). The practice of requiring women's resignation on marriage (the 'marriage bar') did not, then, operate strictly from the first for women factory inspectors.

Organisation of the Women's Branch

Following the organisational change of 1896, some considerable stability in the arrangements for the women inspectors was achieved:

" Staff Committees to enquire into and make recommendations on organisation came and went at intervals of a few years, but the only important changes affecting organisation of the women inspectors' work that came before 1921 were in 1899 and 1908. In 1899 came the useful devolution, never extended beyond 2 districts, of special district charge of certain women's industries into the women inspectors' hands. In the later year came the creating of new group centres in the chief industrial cities, where the women inspectors, under charge of a senior woman, carried on their routine general inspection and enquiries into complaints ... but with newly defined duties, investigating notified cases of industrial poisoning, accidents and other matters specially affecting women. All this work was subject to ... central direction ... through the Principal Woman Inspector, and was carried on in definitely regulated co-operation with their colleagues, the men inspectors in charge of Districts, as well as the medical and engineering inspectors. " (Anderson, 1922 p14)

The reorganisation of 1908 seems to have been one to which Miss Anderson expressed some opposition, and McFeely claims that she saw the establishment of regional centres for the Women's Branch as undermining her own position and authority. She was not a member of the Committee which recommended the changes, and was unsuccessful in her attempts to delay them. Her senior staff, who gained a supervisory role for themselves, and some autonomy, by these changes, seem however to have greeted the change with some enthusiasm.

" The new district supervisors were so eager to establish themselves that they moved faster than clerical help and office space could be arranged. Rose Squire, unwilling to wait for suitable accommodations, began running her district from a one-room office she shared with three other inspectors and a clerk. There was no typewriter, and almost no furniture, and papers were piled up on the floor, but, pleased with her new authority, she went to work enthusiastically. " (McFeely, 1988 p116-7)

Chapter Two

The work of the first women inspectors 1893-1913

The details of the work and achievements of the women inspectors are to be found, above all, in the detailed annual reports of the Principal Lady Inspector. While the full range of their work, which grew with the expansion of the Women's Branch, cannot be indicated here, some aspects are of particular importance. In carrying out their duties, the early women inspectors displayed dedication and enormous energy, often working to the limits of what was humanly possible, and to the cost of their own health. They were motivated by considerations of social justice, compassion and human dignity.

The work of enforcing the law on women's hours of employment and of implementing the Truck Acts took up much of their time. Equally important were their efforts to reduce accidents and to combat hazards such as industrial poisoning. The regulation of work in laundries was especially important.

Women's hours of employment

Their special responsibility for enforcing the law as regards the employment of women and young persons meant that the early women inspectors were closely involved in checking the length of the working day in the industries in which women and girls were employed. As Hilda Martindale, who began work as an inspector in 1902, points out in her book *From one generation to another*:

❝ The hours of employment permissible under the Factory Acts in 1901 were long. Women and girls over 14 years could be employed 12 hours a day with $1\frac{1}{2}$ hours for meals, and on Saturday 8 hours, with half an hour as an interval. In addition, in certain industries, and dressmaking was one, an additional 2 hours could be worked on 30 nights in any 12 months. Hence it was legal to employ women from 8 am to 10 pm. Sunday work was not allowed. ❞ (Martindale, 1944 p74-5)

The inspection of factories and workshops to ensure the correct observance of the law as regards hours of employment thus formed an important part of the women inspectors' duties. In many instances it was for breaches of the law in this respect that employers were prosecuted. Adelaide Anderson, in her memoir *Women in the factory*, recalled:

❝ I may confess that my own first feelings were chiefly of consternation on learning that I had, a few weeks after entering the Department, personally to prosecute an occupier for illegal employment of girls - never having previously entered a police court. I suggested to the District Inspector that he might conduct the first one, just 'to show how it was done', but fortunately and wisely he declined. ❞ (Anderson, 1922 p201-2)

Hilda Martindale recounts an incident of inspection which gives an idea of the persistence and enthusiasm which earned the women inspectors their early high reputation.

❝ An exciting Sunday I spent still lives in my memory. An anonymous complaint had been received that the women employed in a well-known workshop were to be employed on Sunday. I visited at 11 am on that day, but was kept waiting before the front door was opened. On reaching the workrooms I found them empty. But the windows were open, and the covers placed over the work gave the appearance of having been put there in haste. On a previous visit I had obtained the names and addresses of some of the workers, so I hailed a hansom cab and drove to Brixton and Balham - the dormitories for the West End workers - only to hear at their homes that they were at work. Back I drove to the workshop, hoping this time I might obtain an immediate entry, as a second visit from an Inspector would hardly be expected. I met, however, the same fate, and the workrooms were once again empty. In the evening I returned to Brixton and Balham and found the workers at home and was told with excitement how they had been hustled into their employer's bathroom in his house adjoining the workshop at each of my visits. I had the comfort of hearing that my activities had thoroughly disorganised the day's work, and the declarations I took from the workers resulted in a successful prosecution. ❞ (Martindale, 1944 p75)

Small wonder that in 1910 the historians of factory legislation, B L Hutchins and A Harrison, should write of the appointment of women inspectors:

Miss Rose Squire, appointed Lady Inspector 27 Oct 1895

66 Their appointment has been attended with undoubted success, and they deserve much credit for the zeal they have shown in securing an effective administration of the Factory Acts. 99 (Hutchins and Harrison 1966 p249)

Indeed, even as early as 1901, the women inspectors received and investigated 288 reports of illegal employment, the largest single category of the reports received. Their investigations that year led to 58 prosecutions for illegal employment.

That such illegal employment and the need for ingenious inspection of this aspect of the law

continued for some years at the start of the century is shown by other examples in the official record, although in her report for the year 1910 Miss Anderson does note 'there seem to have been improvements in the dressmaking and laundry trades'. (ARCI ,1910 p130)

One example quoted by Miss Paterson highlighted the inadequacy of the law with regard to:

66 such as many of the workers in various despatch rooms, those who fold newspapers or magazines, or make into packets Christmas cards and picture postcards, if no manufacturing process takes place on the premises. The hours of these are often very long and the work generally intermittent. In one case where a very long spell of work prevailed, it was found that the young persons could not even have the protection of the Shop Hours Act, for the picture postcards were not being put together for sale in a shop or warehouse, but were to be hawked from door to door. 99 (ARCI, 1910 p130)

The taking home of work after the end of legally limited hours in the factory was a problem which the women confronted on many occasions. Miss Squire reported from inspection in Somerset in 1907:

66 In Taunton there are several shirt and collar factories giving employment to hundreds of women and girls. It has been for some years the custom there to close the factories (except during the very busy season) at 6 or 7 pm, and to give the employees work to take home, which they bring back in the morning finished. Women and girls were working in their own homes late at night and early in the morning in order to complete the work brought out after a day's work in the factory. Visiting the homes, girls were found at work on linen collars or fronts which were lying heaped on chairs or tables. The

employers were cautioned, and as compliance was promised in all but one case, only one firm was prosecuted. The girls hold different opinions on the matter. Some desire earnestly to be protected from the strain of 'never knowing when you have done' which work taken home involves, others resent any interference with their liberty to earn more money by work done after hours, not seeing as others do that the piece-work rate is depressed by the system. 99 (ARCI, 1907 p183)

This contradiction, between the inspectors' perception of workers' welfare, and workers' own judgements, was to arise frequently in the work of the women inspectors.

Employment of women before and after childbirth

Another area for which the women inspectors had special responsibility was the enforcement of the law concerning the employment of women before and after childbearing. This was another difficult area of the law, and there are numerous mentions in the annual reports of the need to tighten up the legislation. Miss Anderson was well aware of the difficulty of reaching a satisfactory solution to this problem. In 1907 she wrote about the employment of women in the weeks before and after childbirth, a practice which employers were not allowed 'knowingly' to permit:

66 The many sidedness of the problem of regulating the employment of mothers in industry becomes ever clearer. Mere enforcement of the prohibition of such employment, unaccompanied by benefit funds (coupled with some control over the wages of the deserting fathers) in many cases necessarily inflicts increased suffering on the mothers, and if fully enforceable would, without such funds, be liable to introduce new evils. Even if the prohibition were made effectual by removal of the word 'knowingly' from section 61 it would need for its effectual working some system of registration and medical certificates .... Requirement of a medical certificate before resumption of her work, after confinement, such as is found in several European codes, would do something towards preventing the present general evasion of responsibility in the matter. 99 (ARCI, 1907 p184)

On the same question, Miss Paterson commented,

66 Nothing ... demonstrates more thoroughly the value of legislative restriction than a series of visits to employed mothers, and consideration of all the evils that result. With work for women as easy to obtain as it has been of late, while the supply of unskilled labouring men is so much greater than the demand for their labour, one cannot blame the woman for doing what seems to her the only possible thing, however much one may blame the employer who says he took her back too soon out of kindness. I have visited during the year many homes where the mother was the chief, sometimes the only, breadwinner, and have been struck by the extent to which the women realise the value of the exclusion 'if they could live during the time'. Unfortunately it is just when she is least fit to work

Hosiery finishing: trimming army socks

that she most requires money, and I know of no more pathetic and tragic figure than that of the toil-worn woman striving, however ineffectually, to do the work of two persons with, as her background, the unemployed or insufficiently employed man. " (ARCI, 1907 p104)

The implementation of the Truck Acts

The Truck Acts comprised a body of legislation designed to eradicate the practice of paying workers in the form of goods or credit. The legislation enforced by the early women inspectors dated from as far back as 1831, but also included new legislation in the form of the Truck Act 1896. Rose Squire, whose adventures in Ireland and the south west of England in pursuit of offenders against this body of legislation have been recorded both in her own book *Thirty years in the public service* and by McFeely (1988), is perhaps the best source of summary comment on this topic. To her, the Truck Acts were intended to:

" prevent the employer exploiting his workers - whether weavers or coalminers, or employees in any other trade - by making them take as wages goods from the shop kept by him for that purpose and known in some districts as the 'tommy shop'. " (p78)

Squire recalls how in rural Ireland women were employed as knitters and embroiderers by Belfast firms operating through 'middleman' shopkeepers, known somewhat quaintly as 'the gombeen man'. She notes:

" However urgent the need for money might be, tea - on which the shopkeeper made a large profit - was the only reward their labour could obtain. Bitter were the complaints which reached the Government on the peasants' behalf, but they themselves were so terrified of the employers that until a woman inspector was sent from London, to spend some weeks among them as a tourist and win their confidence by chatting in cabins and on the roadside, no sufficient evidence on which to base proceedings could be obtained. In Somerset the same kind of wage-slavery was found to exist among the home-workers making gloves in the villages and in Cornwall among fishermen's wives knitting jerseys on the rocky shores of many a picturesque bay." (Squire, p79)

district seethed with discontent at the truck system and groaned under the tyranny of the 'gombeen man'." (p85-6)

One account from her story of how infringements of the Acts were detected, witnesses found, evidence gathered, and prosecutions brought merits recounting here. Having had her first prosecution of a particular case dismissed 'on legal grounds', with several of the magistrates 'dissociating

Hosiery finishing: Trimming stockings

Squire recalls how after 'the position in Donegal had been reconnoitred in the first instance by Dame Adelaide Anderson' (p85) she was herself sent to Ireland to gather evidence and information.

" Equipped with bicycle, camera, sketch-book and sandwiches, I spent my days at first roaming the country, conversing by the roadside, on the moors and in the cabins with women and girls, who were always ceaselessly knitting and always welcomed and opened their hearts to the English lady. There was no doubt about it, the whole

themselves from this decision' (p95), Squire was instructed to bring fresh proceedings. Many of her witnesses had been interfered with and frightened into withdrawing their evidence, but in February 1900, the case came forward once more:

" During the hearing of these cases the court was the scene of an indescribable tumult. The defending solicitor fiercely attacked the presiding stipendiary magistrate, and demanded his withdrawal from the bench ... and (finally) called the chairman 'a liar'."

The bench was forced to withdraw, but on resumption of the case:

" The utmost confusion prevailed, several persons talking at once and each raising his voice louder to drown the other. The defendant insisted on so frequently interrupting his own solicitor, that at last the exasperated lawyer sat upon his client, not metaphorically but physically, using his elbows alternately to push back the protesting head that appeared first on one side and then on the other of the eloquent advocate. " (pp95-6)

This case ultimately went to Dublin to the High Court, where Squire records 'judgement, alas! went against us'.

" This placed Irish homeworkers and outworkers outside the protection of the Truck Acts owing to the legal necessity ... that in every case it must be proved that there was a contract of service with the worker that he or she should personally execute the work. This interpretation of the law ... proved a serious obstacle in the path of reform, which had steadily been gaining ground as a consequence of the convictions obtained in the earlier cases ... in other parts of Ireland. The Truck system had, however, received a serious check from the publicity given to it, and workers, emboldened to ask for money payment, obtained it. " (pp96-7)

Miss Squire at least had the satisfaction of high praise in the Chief Inspector's Annual Report for 1899, when he commented:

" Nothing could exceed the courage and ability displayed by the Lady Inspector in circumstances of altogether exceptional difficulty. " (ARCI, 1899)

The attempts to enforce the Truck Acts of 1831 and 1887 centred on the illegal payment of wages in kind: but as the annual reports of the Principal Lady Inspector make clear, there were other 'truck' abuses which also needed investigating and eliminating. The main area with which the women inspectors were concerned was the system of fines and deductions from wages which was quite widespread in the late nineteenth century, especially where workers were badly paid and unorganised. Women workers were particularly vulnerable to exploitation through these practices.

Miss Paterson took great exception to the practice which she found widespread in Manchester clothing and garment factories of 'raffling' damaged goods. She comments somewhat sanctimoniously:

" ... I consider that its effect is exceedingly bad. Leaving aside altogether the effect on character of gambling even to so slight an extent, I think it tends to make workers careless in their work; to make foremen and employers careless about training good workers, and indifferent to 'fairness' when they assess damage which is not to be paid for by the worker, probably young and inexperienced, who actually did it, but is to be levied from as many workers as the number of the pennies they claim. The compulsory purchase by the worker of damaged work is, as the Truck Act becomes better understood, less frequently found as part of the contract, but there is no doubt but the practice of 'giving' the worker or 'allowing' her to take the damaged work for which she already had a deduction made from her wages or has made a payment to her employer, is very prevalent, and is contrary to the intention of the Act. " (ARCI, 1906 p239)

Miss Vines (an inspector since May 1899) gives a detailed account of cases with which she had been involved in 1906. In the Potteries, she had found widespread use of deductions from wages for a wide variety of reasons:

> 66 In this district so many charges, such as those for the washing of overalls and head-coverings, the use of gas, the sweeping of floors, etc, are made to the workers. For instance, the following is a list of the weekly deductions made from a majolica paintress, who earned on an average 11s a week:

Washing of overalls and cap	3d
Stamping firm's number on tile	3d
Cooking (when done)	2d
Mess-room	2d
Lavatories	1d
Sweeping and hot water	3d
	1s 2d

> The girl was also frequently stopped, ie deductions were made, for what the firm designated 'defective work'. 99 (ARCI, 1906 p243)

Miss Vines had had some success in dealing with Truck offences in London:

> 66 ...a poor outworker living at Walthamstow, was unfairly deducted 11s 6d for work which she had not spoilt. I saw the manager of the firm in south London for whom she worked, who agreed to refund the money and sent the woman a postal order for 11s 6d on the day of my visit. 99 (ARCI, 1906 p245)

Not all the employers on the receiving end of Miss Vines' critical comments were so compliant with her wishes. In breweries, she found the use, in one month, of fines 'for bad work', without contract or the giving of written particulars:

A)	Not smelling bottles after washing	6d
B)	Paraffin bottle in soaking tank	6d
C)	Leaving off slips and bad labelling	3d
D)	Missing carbolic stopper	6d
E)	Bad sighting	3d
F)	Not smelling stoppers	3d
G)	Oil in soaking tank	6d
H)	Not smelling stoppers	6d
I)	Not smelling stoppers	3d
J)	Not smelling stoppers	3d

> 66 In addition to the above, fines for late arrival were made without contract, written particulars or the keeping of a fine register ... at another brewery, Miss Squire and I found that a bottle-washer had been fined 2s 6d for not detecting the presence of a dead mouse in a bottle. It is well-nigh impossible, owing to the rate the girls have to work at the machines, for them to discover the carcase of a mouse in a black bottle, and I was glad to hear from one firm that, as a safeguard against mice being again found in bottled beer, they had ordered that no beer at any of their branches should again be bottled in black bottles and that in future only white or green bottles would be employed. It is much to be wished that this practice might be universally adopted. 99 (ARCI, 1906 p245)

The Annual Report of 1907 is interesting on Truck offences because it indicates the extent to which continued vigilance was necessary in upholding the law. Miss Squire returned to Somerset where she had investigated truck offences at the turn of the century. She explains:

> 66 A complaint was received ... that outworkers employed in glove-making in Somersetshire were being paid in grocery, contrary to the Truck Act. With Miss Slocock's assistance I investigated and

Asbestos workers

found the complaint justified. The two agents for giving out the gloves to be done in the homes, who also kept shops, were the same two whom I dealt with in 1900. One of them was convicted and fined for paying wages in grocery that year. Miss Slocock and I visited a number of the outworkers, and their evidence was clear that the Truck system, which was in abeyance for a little while after that prosecution in 1900, gradually revived, and for the last few years had been quite as much practiced as before ... The provisions of the Truck Act of 1831 are still needed, and unless the hands of the inspectors are strengthened to deal with outworkers (as recommended by the Lord Chief Justice in Squire v Midland Lace company), Truck may increase. " (ARCI, 1907 p196)

Industrial poisoning and disease

Adelaide Anderson was rightly proud of the role played by the women inspectors in investigating and controlling women's and young people's exposure to industrial poisoning and disease. Although it was not until the reorganisation of 1909 that the women inspectors were formally accorded the primary responsibility of 'investigating notified cases of industrial poisoning, accidents and other matters concerning women' (Anderson, 1922 p14), as she indicates:

" We had already, before 1900, a wide knowledge of the conditions under which lead, phosphorous and mercurial poisoning had occurred, and had brought to light unreported cases, particularly of lead and phosphorous necrosis, and some secondary effects of lead poisoning in women. " (Anderson, 1922 p115)

For example, the women inspectors' report to the Chief Inspector for 1897 included an analysis of 'the 404 cases of lead poisoning reported within the

Asbestos workers

year ended March 31st 1897 from 132 factories in North Staffordshire employing 3040 persons in lead processes'. (ARCI, 1897 p9I)

In the following year, complaints submitted led to the investigation of mercurial poisoning in hatters' furriers' works, and arrangements were afterwards made for Miss Deane and Miss Squire to visit all factories in the country engaged in this trade (ARCI, 1898), which was previously outside the group of trades classified as dangerous. As Harrison has pointed out, the investigations of the women inspectors 'often resulted in new trades being regulated, as in 1898, with the use of mercury by hatters and furriers'. (Harrison, 1990 p81)

Asbestos

Perhaps even more importantly, given the serious danger to health which this substance was later to be found to pose, in that same year, 1898, Miss Deane noted:

66 The evil effects of asbestos dust have also attracted my attention. A microscopic inspection of this mineral dust which was made by H M Medical Inspector clearly revealed the sharp, glass-like, jagged nature of the particles, and where they are allowed to rise and to remain suspended in the air of a room, in any quantity, the effects have been found to be injurious, as might have been expected ... In dusty trades the worker may continue for a very long time apparently unaffected, before the symptoms of the evil become marked. 99 (ARCI, 1898)

Again in 1899, the annual report draws attention to investigation of the 'effects on health of asbestos dust', this time by Miss Paterson. Among the processes mentioned was the manufacture of asbestos jacketing for insulating pipes.

A few years later, Anderson repeated her concern about the dangers of asbestos, when she wrote in the annual report of 1906:

66 Of all injurious dusty processes of which I have again in 1906 received repeated complaints, none, I believe, surpass in injuriousness to the workers the sieving, preparing, carding and spinning processes in manufacture of asbestos. The following is a characteristic complaint: 'Asbestos manufacture ... noxious dust from carding engines and breaker. The breaker, colloquially called the "Devil", produces a great deal of dust; there are two fans in the room, but these are not connected with the machines, so that they merely circulate the dust. Girls from 14 upwards look after the machines. A fortnight after the place is swept down the dust lies half an inch thick on the beams'. 99 (ARCI, 1906 p219)

She goes on to give details of the effects on health as observed by Miss Martindale:

66 One woman complained of bronchitis, and a few stated that they suffered from a morning cough ... about 3 weeks ago a spinner died of consumption. Visited her home to enquire and found that she died at 24 years of age after working 6 years as asbestos spinner; for 3 years she had suffered from a morning cough, and for the last 10 months of her life was unable to work; none of her relations had suffered from consumption. 99 (ARCI, 1906 p120)

Doing her best to underline her anxieties she went on:

66 Much time for patient research among workers who have dropped out of this employment is necessary before any true idea can be formed of the effect of the process. 99

Lead

Despite ringing these alarm bells about asbestos, it was perhaps lead poisoning which the women inspectors saw as the most serious threat to the health of women workers.

Harrison claims that the concern about lead poisoning in women and girls had developed following Alexander Redgrave's enquiry into lead poisoning in 1882. She argues that the approach advocated by factory inspectors and others was flawed because it relied upon the use of 'protective' regulation of women's and girls' work and 'a morass of complex rules and regulations, which perhaps unsurprisingly did not seem to be observed' (1989 p181). The simple 'solution' of banning the use of raw lead was not chosen.

Although Harrison is probably right to criticise the focus on 'the idea of susceptibility; ideas about class and poverty, and the idea of individual culpability' at this time, the reports of the women inspectors' activities do show how deeply concerned they were about the welfare of women working with lead, making systematic observations and taking practical action.

The women inspectors who had been involved in the proceedings of the Royal Commission on Labour were already well acquainted with the emerging evidence about the dangers of lead, especially white lead. Indeed, it was one of the motives behind their desire to be factory inspectors. On her first visit to the Dilkes in 1894, Lucy Deane took part in conversations about the hazards of white lead (McFeely, 1988 pp23-4).

Loading yarn in the manufacture of rope

Deane's first inspection of the Staffordshire potteries in 1894 led to the introduction of regulations about ventilation and sanitation in pottery manufacture, where lead was used in some of the processes. But when Deane and Paterson returned in 1897 they found the regulations having little effect: they investigated, and Lucy Deane's diary records that in April and May 1897 they interviewed several dozen female victims of lead poisoning in their hotel in Hanley (McFeely, 1988 p66). Shortly afterwards, J H Tennant, MP, used some of Lucy Deane's case histories of lead poisoning in a parliamentary debate supporting his amendment to the Employer's Liability Bill (ibid). The investigations had revealed a high degree of childlessness, stillbirths and miscarriages among married women employed in lead processes (p116).

Thereafter, pressure mounted for a woman inspector to be permanently stationed in the Potteries. The Women's Trade Union League and a number of Liberal MPs, as well as the Dilkes, pushed hard to achieve this objective. Finally, in 1902, Hilda Martindale was appointed to this (temporary) position. Martindale's clerical work was to be done from London, and she was to stay in the Potteries 'on a

reduced night allowance' (Martindale, 1944 p85). She commented:

66 It was certainly a novel position and not an altogether easy one. The (male) District Inspector was well known in the district and knew the industry in all its aspects. It cannot have been easy for him to have a woman Inspector imposed on him whose standard of work might not be similar to his own. I have to admit that my relationship with him at times was somewhat difficult; but we both tried to work harmoniously together and on the whole succeeded. 99 (Martindale, 1944 p85)

66 I settled down at the North Stafford Hotel, Stoke-on-Trent. I made my bedroom my office, had a special trunk made to hold my papers and hand-copying press, and soon became accustomed to writing out my reports, letters and information forms in copying ink, and to damping the flimsies on the large old-fashioned marble-top washstand. Unfortunately there were no typewriting machines for Inspectors of Factories in those days, and fortunately there was no fixed basin in the bedroom of the hotel. Thus equipped I started work. 99 (Martindale, 1944 p86)

By the time she submitted her report to the Chief Inspector of Factories for the 1904 Annual Report, Martindale was able to claim:

66 I have now visited every factory in England in which women are employed and which are under China and Earthenware Special Rules, with the exception of those at Newcastle-upon-Tyne and one factory at Birmingham. 99 (p87)

She found her investigations fascinating, but the condition of the workers meant that 'the work was painful' (1944 p88). She points out that in the

Miss Hilda Martindale, HM Deputy Chief Inspector of Factories 1925-1933

Jute workers baling

absence of health insurance and workers' compensation, which was not at that time applicable to the trade:

❝ women continued to work long after they were feeling the effects of lead poisoning, knowing that if they gave in there would be no wages coming in. ❞ (p88)

Recalling specific distressing cases, she identified what she saw as the way forward in dealing with lead poisoning:

❝ Scrupulous cleanliness in the work and workplaces, efficient exhaust ventilation for dangerous processes and early diagnosis of the complaint were, I soon realised, the surest way of fighting the dangers of plumbism, and to these I gave special attention. ❞ (p88)

The following year, Miss Martindale was removed from this work and sent to Ireland for the investigation into Truck, somewhat to her regret. Recalling developments in inspecting in the Potteries many years later, she observed:

❝ It was cheering to find that the Special Rules I had helped to administer had meantime become Special Regulations dealing in a very detailed way with the dangers and risks in the trade, and that many of the recommendations I had made had been embodied in them and were coming into force in 1913. Among these was clay-carrying; in future it was to be illegal for any boy or girl to carry more than 30 lb. Also a person had to be appointed in every factory whose duty it was to see to the observance of the Regulations. Such changes marked great progress, as did also the number of lead-poisoning cases, which in 1913 numbered 63 to be reduced by 1939 to 7 cases. In 1942, however, an advance was made which in my wildest dreams in 1905 I had never contemplated;

a woman, Miss Kathleen Crundwell, was appointed District Inspector and was accepted whole-heartedly by the industry. " (p90)

The 'remarkable Pottery Code of Regulations, 1913, which followed on the general lines of drastic recommendations made by the Departmental Committee under Sir Ernest Hatch' (Anderson, 1922 p117-8), arose from investigations in the early years of the century. Both Miss Martindale and Miss Vines gave evidence to the Hatch Committee. They could report:

" the distressing fact that in 1906 there were 107 cases of lead poisoning reported in earthenware and china works, as compared with 84 in 1905 - a rise of 23 cases, of which four, or one more than in 1905, terminated fatally ... " (ARCI, 1906 p213)

Miss Anderson notes:

" Miss Vines ... constantly receives complaints from the manufacturers of the impossibility of carrying out the Special Rules. She urges that if they adhere to this position it necessarily presses forward the question of the use of leadless glazes, and ... she has been led to discuss with them the practicability of development of the use of leadless glazes. " (ARCI, 1906 p217-8)

The difficulties involved in developing such glaze are then recounted by Miss Vines in some detail.

The following year, Adelaide Anderson draws special attention to the achievements in combating industrial poisoning and diseases, noting her own involvement, with the Medical Inspector, in the production and publication of the *Joint Report on Tinning of Metals*, and the submission of recommendations from her staff for the conversion of Earthenware and China Rules into Regulations. Miss

Vines' 'steady 4 months' work' in the North Staffordshire Potteries is reported. She notes that cases of plumbism are falling more rapidly for girls and women than for boys and men:

" From one point of view this is encouraging, but ... an increase of illness among the men necessitates a larger number of women leaving their homes and going out to work. For instance, I noted one day, on inspection of a tile works, a majolica paintress looking particularly white and ill. Visiting her in the dinner hour I found she had only been confined two months before, and besides the baby there were 2 other small children and a sick husband. The man,

Packing rope for the Navy

aged 31, had been a dipper and had, he said, been suffering from lead poisoning for about 3 years. Up till a few months previously he had been receiving compensation weekly, but then owing to the expenses connected to his wife's confinement he had been forced to accept a lump sum of £35 down. When I saw him he was still ill and his right wrist so weak that he could not lift a kettle. The wife, therefore, though far from strong and probably without sufficient food, was obliged to work daily at the factory and earn, so far as it was possible, a living for her husband, her children and herself. 99 (ARCI, 1907 p169)

Miss Vines goes on to draw special attention to what she sees as the key problems, including: 'dust, compensation, high temperatures predisposing to lead poisoning, heavy weights predisposing to lead poisoning'. (ibid)

Jute rope walk

Phosphorus

In 1898 Rose Squire and others undertook an investigation into the manufacture of 'lucifer matches', in which wooden splints were dipped into a paste containing white or yellow phosphorus (Squire, 1927 pp54-58). Inhalation of the fumes from this process, or at other points in the manufacture and packaging of non-safety matches (then in widespread use) was already known to cause phosphorus necrosis.

This very unpleasant disease, known colloquially as 'phossy jaw', had various effects, but its 'most characteristic and terrible manifestation' was inflammation and decay of the jaw bone.

Dangers in match manufacture had been recognised some years before, and some protective measures had been included in the Factory Act 1878 and in Special Rules introduced in 1892.

Unfortunately, these were both insufficient and poorly observed. The trade employed predominantly female and youthful labour.

In 1898, concerned that cases of phosphorus necrosis were being 'hushed up', and that further measures were urgently required, Rose Squire began an investigation in what seemed to her 'the most miserable places I had ever seen'. Now she was to discover just how the 'ugly and ineffective general methods of the business' were damaging workers' health:

❝ I dug out cases of men and women hidden away in the slums - piteous cases they were. Some of the sufferers had toothless gums. One woman had completely lost the lower jaw, a young girl in an earlier stage of the disease was constantly in great pain while the suppurating jaw bone was gradually decaying. The difficulty of taking food, and the prolonged suffering and the resulting disfigurement made the disease a particularly distressing one. No compensation could at that time be claimed for disablement due to industrial disease, and while in the more recent cases some meagre relief (I will not call it hush money!) was paid by the employer, the older sufferers had not received any assistance. ❞ (ARCI, 1907 p169)

Her investigations led to 'immediate' further action. Scientists and medical officers were brought in, and a thorough study of the disease and of measures against it was conducted. This resulted in legal enforcement of fume exhaustion systems and of measures to promote workers' cleanliness, as well as a system of medical and dental examination and care. Some of the worst factories were 'squeezed out' as these new measures were enforced, but Squire later wrote proudly of this work:

❝ The history of the change effected in this industry by legislation should put fresh heart into every social reformer. It is worthy of a prominent place in the annals of the Home Office. ❞ (ARCI, 1907 p169)

Laundries

The inspection of conditions in laundries was important among the activities of the early women inspectors because it gave them the opportunity to acquire expertise and experience in the safe use of machinery and to acquaint themselves with the problems of fencing.

As early as 1895, the joint report of the Women Inspectors' Department noted that the extension of the Act of 1895 to include laundries was 'welcomed by employees' (ARCI, 1895 p121). This 'extension' gave what Hutchins and Harrison have called 'miserably inadequate protection' (1966 p195) under Clause 22 of the Factory Act of 1895. This fixed the weekly limit of hours at 30 for children, 60 for women and young persons, but allowed in a single day 10 hours' work by children, 12 by young persons and 14 by women.

By 1900 there was in the annual reports detailed comment on conditions in laundries, and reference to the 'recent development of specialised laundry machinery'. (ARCI, 1900 p377)

Fencing of laundry machinery

The women inspectors were receiving reports of accidents to women working in laundries: Miss Deane received 37 such reports in the year 1900/1901. Women inspectors were not normally responsible for inspecting and giving guidance on the fencing of machinery: this was a responsibility which they had been encouraged to pass to the male inspectors in the districts. But developments in laundry work, which was overwhelmingly a female trade, gave them the opportunity to extend their skills as inspectors in ways that would later stand them in good stead when the Women's Branch was amalgamated into the general inspectorate.

Miss Norah Curry, an inspector from 1941 to 1976:

❝ has noted the coincidence that very shortly after women took over responsibility for assigned areas where women were mainly employed, the introduction of machinery into laundries began. The women inspectors were thus in a strong position to see the effects of accidents and to advise about precautions. I think this activity in laundries was extremely important in extending the knowledge of the women inspectors leading to the development in their work towards equality of duties with the district male inspectors. ❞

At pains to secure this area of work for women inspectors, in 1900 Miss Anderson asked Miss Deane to arrange to be accompanied by a (woman) colleague on all her visits to laundries where accidents had occurred in order to emphasise:

❝ the responsibility of every member of the women Inspector's Branch for noting dangers in machinery, just as if the sole responsibility for ordering the guard were assigned to them. ❞ (ARCI, 1900 p377)

Miss Anderson reported, as usual, in the Annual Report of 1907. Now she was able cautiously to note:

❝ It is satisfactory that the normal increase in substitution of power driven machinery for hand processes is not accompanied by a pro rata increase of accidents attributable to the machinery. Though fencing does not everywhere progress as we would wish it to do, we yet seem to be slowly gaining ground. ❞ (ARCI, 1907 p161)

Her comments are accompanied by Table B indicating causes of laundry accidents:

A. Laundry accidents: Incidence according to sex 1903-07

Year	Persons employed in registered laundries		Accidents 1903		1904		1905		1906		1907	
	M	F	M	F	M	F	M	F	M	F	M	F
	(1)	(2)	(3)	(4)	(5)	(6)	(7)	(8)	(9)	(10)	(11)	(12)
1901...	8434	82 652	43	252	42	262	57	219	46	255	60	319
1904...	10 480	93 997										

source ARCI, 1907 p161

Causation		United Kingdom 1901-1907							Miss Sadler's Area 1901-1907						
		-01	-02	-03	-04	-05	-06	-07	-01	-02	-03	-04	-05	-06	-07
Indrawing heated rollers	Calenders and multiple roller ironers	79	85	55	49	44	49	63	7	13	6	4	4	4	6
	Rollers impinging on a board (shirt and collar machines)	59	53	81	89	53	70	89	4	5	4	8	3	4	6
	Body linen ironers with movable upper arm	10	14	12	21	19	32	15	-	3	3	4	5	2	1
Indrawing cold rollers -- wringers and starchers		85	72	81	74	66	61	73	8	14	7	12	5	9	9
Traversing part of machine	Box mangle	2	1	11	13	5	6	10	1	2	-	2	3	5	3
	Shirt and collar machines	-	6	3	5	6	2	16	-	-	1	-	-	-	2
Hydro-extractors	Revolving cage	11	11	11	7	10	14	16	1	3	-	1	2	1	-
	Gear and friction cones	3	2	3	2	3	1	3	2	-	-	-	-	-	-
Washing machines	Rotary cage	5	6	4	4	4	8	9	-	2	1	-	-	-	1
	Lid and gear	1	2	4	4	8	7	9	1	-	1	-	1	2	1
Hoists		-	-	1	4	2	3	3	-	-	1	1	1	3	1
Engines etc - fly-wheel		1	1	1	-	1	4	7	-	-	-	-	1	-	1
Other mill gearing	Main shaft, belts, pulleys etc	7	9	6	11	17	2	8	-	1	2	-	3	-	-
	Gearing accessory to machines	9	6	7	4	10	13	8	-	-	2	-	-	2	4
Scalds		5	10	6	6	16	14	24	1	1	1	1	1	-	3
Burns		4	1	3	2	1	3	7	-	-	-	-	-	-	-
Blows, falls etc		8	9	6	3	9	11	16	1	-	-	1	5	-	1
Fan		-	-	-	6	2	1	3	-	-	-	-	1	-	-
		289	288	295	304	276	301	379	26	44	29	34	35	32	39

source ARCI, 1907 p161

More satisfaction still emerges from the annual report of 1910. The Act of 1907 was working well as regards hours:

66 and there seems to be a general preference among employers for the system. 99 (ARCI, 1910 p131)

Institution laundries

An interesting aspect of the women's work at this time concerns their attempts to improve conditions in what were termed 'institution' laundries. Although under the 1901 Factory and Workshop Consolidation Act such laundries were exempt from inspection, the 1902 Annual Report indicates that 204 institutions were offered visits by inspectors. These (mainly religious and penitentiary) institutions remained a cause of concern to the inspectors despite their special legal status: in 1905, 'special concentration of attention' was given to institutional laundries, factories and workshops (ARCI, 1906 p186), and the following year Miss Tracey and Miss Martindale both visited institutions. Miss Tracey reports:

66 The one dread in all the homes seems to be that government inspection may mean a slackening of discipline and a loosening of the moral hold the superiors have over the inmates. That is, I think, an imaginary danger, for every

Lace workers with teacher

inspector must sympathise with the aim of the homes to improve the life and strengthen the moral fibre of these unfortunate girls ... I suppose the silent system has certain advantages ... otherwise it would not be so generally in vogue, but in the one home I saw in which it had not existed for some years, the atmosphere was altogether different and homelike. ... The extreme youth of the inmates is a very distressing feature. Laundry work must, I suppose, be held to be peculiarly suited to the temperament of the inmates, for it is so universally adopted, but on the face of it it does not appear to offer any deep human interest ... ,,

Miss Martindale reported from Scotland her concerns about fire hazards, inadequate fencing of machinery, low dietary standards, the use of profits, and the management of such institutions, commenting:

,, it was an extremely difficult matter to impress the matrons in charge of the danger to which the workers were subjected. ,, (ARCI, 1906 p186-7)

The work done to enquire into the conditions in these institutional laundries was influential in determining some of the detailed provisions of the Laundries Act 1907. This Act brought laundries under the ordinary law for non-textile factories and workshops, although permitting some variation in the hours of women's employment. Overtime after 9 o'clock at night was banned under the Act, and laundries 'carried on as auxiliary to another business or incidentally to the purposes of any public institution' came within its remit. The Act also stated that 'charitable and reformatory laundries' were to be inspected by factory inspectors (Hutchins and Harrison, 1966 p256).

Institution laundries had mostly accepted the visits of factory inspectors, if sometimes with reluctance, and here Miss Tracey reported:

❝ a great advance in social order; the conditions are less harassing, and the girls' clothing tidier and less repellently ugly than it used to be. One encouraging sign is the almost complete disappearance of the old nomenclature - 'Home for Penitent Females', and such like, so that the girls are no longer under the disadvantage of being labelled when leaving. I think I may say that all the fencing of machinery is in a satisfactory condition ... The improvement in the cleanliness of the laundries is very marked. Ventilation is also better, but what is most striking is the improvement in the temperature of the ironing room, due to the removal or effectual screening of the stove. ❞ (ARCI, 1910 p131)

A pioneering role,
a compassionate approach

The early women inspectors showed their concern for the conditions of working class women in their choice of career and in some cases in their political activities too. Once in post as factory inspectors they made it their business to use their sex to get closer to women workers' problems than they, and their advocates, believed it was possible for male inspectors to do. They visited women workers who had been injured or who had fallen sick or made complaints in their homes. They also showed genuine concern for women's welfare in some of their activities, sometimes on an individual basis, and maintained and fostered links with the leaders of the women's unions.

In 1906 Miss Slocock visited workshops for unemployed women, 'opened by the Central Unemployed Body for London'. Miss Anderson noted that these were for women who were '(a) either widows or (b) whose husbands are unable to work through illness or infirmity or (c) obliged by some other cause unforeseen to be breadwinners'. Miss Slocock commented:

❝ The interesting point economically about these women was that they were not in any sense skilled workers ... the majority were women who had done casual work, such as charring, housework, washing by the day and some of whom

Harnessing jacquard frame

C. Sources of complaints 1906

Sources	1906	1905	1904
Anonymous	362	440	378
Signed by workers or their friends	303	296	187
From organisations:			
a. Women's Trade Union League and various Trade Unions	155	137	73
b. Industrial Law Committee, Women's Industrial Council and Christian Social Union	114	131	129
c. Women's Settlements	25	6	2
From public officials:			
a. Central	101	105	26
b. Local	28	52	156
Total	1 088	1 167	951

source ARCI, 1906 p191

were now living in a neighbourhood where there was little demand for this class of work. ❞ (ARCI, 1906 p187)

That same year, the report notes as an important source of complaints about working conditions the women's trade unions. Table C shows that complaints from this source more than doubled between 1904 and 1906. Boston has commented on the links between the women inspectors and the women's union representatives:

❝ The women trade unionists had good allies in those first few women factory inspectors. They were outspoken women of courage who gave untiring devotion to their work. The annual reports of the women factory inspectors provided authoritative evidence which was a powerful weapon in the campaign for greater protection of women workers. ❞   (Boston, 1980 p36)

The compassionate approach which the women inspectors took to the many social problems which they encountered in the course of inspection comes through very clearly in the detailed individual accounts which are such an interesting feature of the annual reports of the years before 1914. A few examples can illustrate this aspect of their approach, while also indicating the nature and extent of some of the problems of working people which they encountered. Their investigations included many visits to workers in their homes, and their reports give ample indication of their sympathy for workers suffering from harsh working conditions.

Lace-making

Miss Squire, who had been inspecting the lace trade in Nottingham, where 'very serious contraventions' had been discovered, reported in 1906:

❝ The lace drawing and clipping is a notoriously badly sweated industry. I visited several most sad homes this week ... where the father is out of work and the mother and children are slaving away at lace for which from ¹/₂d to 2¹/₂d per dozen yards of from 6 to 12 breadths is paid. ❞   (ARCI, 1906 p229)

Nearby, she found a girl of 13 with defective eyesight drawing lace in a workshop (in which

Lace worker operating a plain net machine

Lace workers - the finished article

premises no examination by a certifying surgeon was required). She had been 'excused school' on account of her eyesight. Miss Squire continues:

66 This girl was drawing lace. I visited her home; her mother is a widow struggling with the poorly paid lace-clipping at home, while the little girl has for a year been working at the workshop. They begged me not to interfere ... I could suspend her under Section 67, but I feel sure the occupiers would dismiss her, and she would then escape the medical examination, and probably get into another workshop or do the same kind of work at home. 99 (ARCI, 1906 p229)

Employment of married women

Much concern is expressed by the inspectors about the employment of women after childbearing; sometimes this extends into a general moral objection to the employment of married women. Adelaide Anderson comments:

66 From district after district the report reaches me that employment of married women is increasing, and that the evils resulting therefrom

remain continuous in effect. ... enough is known to connect the phenomenon of industrial employment of child-bearing women with local lack of employment for men, or prevalence of casual employment for men. 99 (ARCI, 1906 p233)

She refers further to Miss Deane's observations on this matter:

66 The comparative cheapness of women's labour is ... dearly paid for by the nation, and a system of insurance in aid of the working mothers, which would mitigate this attendant evil, is a charge which might perhaps be profitably attached to the employment of such labour. 99

Going on, she gives most interesting details about arrangements in creches for working mothers in Paris, Baden, Vienna, Berlin, Warsaw, Sofia, Copenhagen, Stockholm and Odessa, taken from a 1904 report of the London County Council entitled *Creches and Day Nurseries*.

Adelaide Anderson was very sympathetic to the position of those desperate women who returned to employment shortly after childbearing. In her evidence to the Inter-Departmental Committee on

Overhead travelling crane

Physical Deterioration, which reported in 1904, she resisted the idea that the period around childbirth when women might not be employed should be extended from one to three months, and pointed out:

  ❝ You have to think of the number that you may expose to the greater misery of starvation (paragraph 1594). You do certainly drive them out upon charity or upon the rates if you prohibit them from employment (paragraph 1601). It is very desirable that the women who are mothers should be kept out of the factory (paragraph 1604) ... but with regard to compulsion to keep them out, I think to force them on charity is rather a serious step. ❞ (paragraph 1605)

She disagreed with the suggestion that there was a 'general tendency' towards the 'excitement and sociability' of factory life preventing a woman settling down when she married and looking after her children, but insisted 'they certainly want companionship and they like to work together.' (paragraph 1622)

Accidents and safety

Some of the most distressing accounts in these annual reports are to be found in the reports of accidents investigated. These include cases, often in laundries, where girls or women had been injured when their hair became entangled in machinery. The consequences of such injury could, as the women inspectors noted, be both physical and psychological: a woman who had been partially or completely scalped would be permanently disfigured. Miss Tracey reported in 1906:

  ❝ A girl of 15 mounted her work table to dust the electric globe to prevent the dust falling on her work, and in turning round her hair was caught on the shafting, causing severe injury to her head and loss of the upper part of scalp. In this case the shafting was 8 feet from the floor, and would not unnaturally be looked upon as quite safe. If in such cases the girls ever recover, their life can be but one of labour and sorrow. ... Until an accident

Lace worker pulling up a catch bar

of this kind has happened, it is difficult to convince any employer of this danger; he merely thinks the Inspector who can press such a matter unnecessarily fussy. 99 (ARCI , 1906 pp206-7)

Whether or not the women inspectors ever were 'unnecessarily fussy' on occasion it is now very difficult to judge, especially since so much of the evidence about their activities comes from their own pens. But it is quite obvious that they were both thorough and meticulous. Commenting in 1910 on sanitary facilities in workplaces, for example, Miss Whitworth remarked:

66 The standard of decency and suitability of sanitary conveniences is low in Lancashire compared with the South. It is there a not uncommon thing to find the women's conveniences without doors, and sometimes without even partitions - they are also situated leading out of rooms where men are employed and side by side with the men's. 99 (ARCI, 1910 p118)

Another of the inspectors' concerns was the carrying of heavy weights and general over-burdening of women and girls in the course of their work. Miss Vines commented of conditions in an earthenware factory in 1906:

66 A manager at one factory remarked to me that he could not understand why the law did not prohibit the carrying of such heavy weights by women. Personally I am of the opinion that for legal restriction to be necessary in England in the twentieth century in order to prevent women and young persons being employed in this way as beasts of burden is not a hopeful sign. I cannot but feel that a moral and not a legal obligation should be sufficient to bring about the cessation of this health-endangering practice. 99 (ARCI, 1906 p223)

Industrial discipline and conduct

In Huddersfield in that same year, Miss Slocock made investigations in the hearth-rug weaving factories. She was not impressed by what she found:

66 It is rough, heavy work, and the trade had got a bad name in the town so that respectable women would not allow their daughters to go into it. ... The workers were all piece-workers and came and went as they chose. The system of fines for being late and of selling the damaged work to the weavers appeared to have been abolished owing to the difficulty of obtaining workers, but there was a lack of discipline and order, and except in the case of one or two workplaces it was entirely in the hands of very rough low-class women. 99 (ARCI, 1906 p190)

The inspectors also took exception to poor treatment of women workers by their employers, ranging from 'bullying' to what would today be termed sexual harassment. In 1906 an attempt is made in the annual report to tabulate complaints 'outside' the Factory and Truck Acts. Among the categories of complaint listed are:

Relating to bad 'living-in' and bedroom arrangements ...7

Trucking waste at a paper mill

Pulping machines

Guillotine cutters

Quality control at a paper mill

Relating to unjust dismissals and 'bullying' of workers (this includes dismissals for refusing to break the law, and harsh treatment for answering inspectors' questions) ...4

Relating to the use of foul language by foremen and immoral influences brought to bear on workers by employers ...4

(ARCI, 1906 p192)

The next year, Miss Anderson comments that:

❝ Complaints relating to conditions of employment or supervision of the work of young women and girls which, directly or indirectly, affect conduct or morality injuriously, have been as in former years important. ... An employer with a sense of responsibility...will warn or reprimand or remove foremen of bad influence or bad language. When the influence or action of the employer himself is bad ... there is no remedy. English law, unlike the codes of some other countries, in no way makes the relations of an employer to the young worker he employs like that of a guardian of good conduct ... ❞ (ARCI, 1907 p151-2)

A more scientific approach

The women inspectors' activities led to praise in a number of quarters. In 1915, an article by Dorothy Haynes appeared in the Women's Industrial News which stated:

❝ The social progress of recent years has been the result of an unprecedented attention to matters of detail. Investigation and administration have begun to go hand in hand, and the scientific spirit which has been so long in coming to its own in matters social may now be said to have arrived ... the great advance which the women inspectors have been able to bring about in factory legislation has been largely due to the sympathetic insight which has made then virtually representative of the people. ❞ (quoted in Anderson, 1922 p200)

The scientific approach was indeed one which the women inspectors had begun to adopt, although by modern standards many of their practices were still somewhat haphazard. In many cases they worked closely with the Medical Inspector, as in the investigations into lead poisoning. In others, they used what scientific instruments they could obtain to measure temperature and humidity in factories and workshops.

Miss Mildred Power, who was appointed in 1905, and had previously been Assistant Bacteriologist to the Royal Commission on Sewage Disposal, seems to have wasted no time in developing her scientific interest in working conditions. In 1906, for example, she sent to Adelaide Anderson a 'summary of the reasons for free ventilation in workrooms, laying special emphasis on its importance in places where gas is supplied for lighting, heating, or motor power'. (ARCI, 1906 p198). She supports her summary with scientific evidence from Prof J Lorraine Smith and Dr Corfield, as well as Prof Glaister, quoting the latter to show that there may be chronic poisoning 'which is very insidious in its onset'. (ARCI, 1906 p198).

The following year Miss Power made

D. Conditions in Dressmakers' workshops in West London

Samples taken 18th December 1906, 6 pm to 8 pm. Barometer, 30.38 (anticyclone); dry bulb 50°F; wet bulb 49°F; humidity, 93 per cent (Glaisher)

Room	Space per head (in cubic feet)	Subjective quality of the air	CO_2, parts per 10 000	Temperature at point where sample was taken			Percentage (Glaisher)	Vapour per cubic foot of the air (grains) (Glaisher)	Vapour required to foot of air (grains) (Glaisher)	Vapour pressure in mercury (Glaisher)	Dew point
				Dry bulb	Wet bulb	Difference					
(Outside air)	-	-	(4)	50°F	49°F	1°F	93	3.8	0.3	0.334	47.9°F
1	650.5	close	14.1	61°F	55°F	6°F	67	4.0	2.0	0.358	49.8°F
2	411	very close	12.4	72°F	62°F	10°F	54	4.7	3.8	0.426	54.5°F
3	368	close	15.9	70°F	61°F	9°F	57	4.6	3.4	0.418	54°F
4	400 (800)	musty, cellar-like smell	12.2	63°F	56°F	7°F	63	4.0	2.4	0.361	50.1°F
Mean values for the four samples	457.3	-	13.6	66.5°F	58.5°F	8°F	60.1	4.3	2.9	0.390	52.1°F

source ARCI, 1907 p 155-6

'very careful observations' in workrooms in the West London district. Adelaide Anderson is at pains to note that 'She summarised the results after fully weighing all the circumstances: (1) weather; (2) subjective test; (3) objective tests, in tables D and E.'

Industrial welfare

Another rather surprising interest in women's conditions of employment is revealed by Hilda Martindale, who in 1907 commented most favourably on the 'employment of women as superintendents and "social secretaries".' In a mill employing '1600 women and children', the manager director had appointed a woman to supervise the health conditions under which the work was carried on, and to undertake the registration of all Home Office requirements. A doctor had also been appointed:

" to attend the mill every week and give advice to the women. Arrangements have been made with the public baths in the neighbourhood to reserve them for a few hours on several afternoons in the week for the use of half-timers in the mill. "

Meals for the children employed, a creche and clubs were all in prospect. In another 'large factory' Martindale reports the appointment of a 'social secretary' with similar duties, and notes that here:

E. *Conditions in Dressmakers' workshops in West London*

Samples taken 18th December 1906, 6 pm to 8 pm. Barometer, 30.38 (anticyclone); dry bulb 50°F; wet bulb 49°F; humidity, 93 per cent (Glaisher)

Room.	Total content in cubic feet.	Persons employed.	Space per head in cubic feet.	CO$_2$, parts per 10 000.	Hygrometric state. (Percentage saturation, Glaisher.)	Air temperature.‡	Wet bulb	Remarks
1	9,758	15	650.5	14.1	67	61°F (65°) mean 63°	55°F	Basement room: Air close; smell of gas (?) from iron heater. Ventilation available: one small window partially open; two doors to adjoining rooms; one stairway to upper floor. Lighting, electric.
2	5,760	14	411	12.4	54	72°F (68°) mean 70°	62°F	Third floor: Air very close. Ventilation available: one window opened immediately before sample taken; 13 windows partially open. 6 incandescent, one ordinary, gas jet alight. Coke fire in use.
3	4,784	13	368	15.9	57	70°F (66°) mean 68°	61°F	Ground floor: Air close. Ventilation available: two ventilators; two windows open. Eight gas jets, 4 feet from floor, alight. Flueless gas stove in use; gas 'kilter' not lighted, but used 'since dinner'.
4	4,000	5 *(10)	800 †(400)	12.2	63	63°F (62°) mean 62.5°	56°F	Basement room: Air musty; smell of cellar. Ventilation available: two small ventilators partially open; staircase leading to upper floor. Fire disused for two hours. Gas ring in use. Lighting, electric.

*   Five persons left the room 40 minutes before sample was taken.
†   Cubic space calculated on usual 10 occupants
‡   Figures not in brackets indicate the dry bulb temperature in spot where air sample was taken.
   Figures in brackets indicate temperature recorded by thermometer in part of room some distance from the spot where the sample was taken.

source ARCI, 1907 p 155-6

“ the workers were given an opportunity of consulting each week a doctor and a dentist.” (ARCI, 1907 p188)

Later, Miss F I Taylor, an inspector for many years, reviewed the early development of welfare in industry, noting:

“In 1909 the first recorded Welfare conference was held and was attended by about 30 employers and welfare workers. In 1913 there was a further conference at which 26 firms were represented, and at the final session an Association of Welfare Workers was also formed.” (ARCI, 1932 p62)

Washing facilities and lavatories

Comparative studies

The other important way in which the early women inspectors contributed to knowledge and understanding of occupational health and safety was through their participation on expert committees, their accumulation of comparative knowledge of employment regulation and protective legislation in other countries, and their participation in international conferences.

In 1894 Adelaide Anderson made summaries of French laws and orders regulating employment, and the following year, 1895, she contributed a lengthy report on German and Austrian industrial codes. As she notes in her book, this was 'before public interest in comparative labour legislation had been awakened.' (1922, p199) Miss Squire was prominently involved in developing this work, which was used to demonstrate the deficiencies of English law in remedying specific complaints:

" For instance, complaints on defective light in the factory, lack of washing conveniences, on heavy weight carrying and dangerous processes. "
(ARCI 1897, 1898, 1804, cited by Anderson, 1922)

In 1899, the Principal Lady Inspector prepared a translation of the regulations in force in Germany to regulate letter press printing (ARCI, 1899), and in 1902 she visited both France and Germany to investigate and report on the law on laundries. In September 1903, she attended, with the Medical Inspector, the International Congress of Hygiene and Demography in Brussels. Here she met Dr Josefa Joteyko, and through this meeting she became interested in studying fatigue prevention (Anderson, 1922 p199). She also gave a paper on the sanitary conditions of workshops, and the powers of local authorities to deal with them (*Inter-Departmental Committee on Physical Deterioration I*, 1904, paragraph 1636, HMSO).

Chapter Three

The First World War and the inter-war years:

new responsibilities, new opportunities

When war broke out on 4 August 1914 Hilda Martindale was on leave with two friends and out of the country. She recalled:

> 66 It was only with difficulty that I reached home in a reasonable time. I used my official position for all it was worth, and after a considerable delay obtained a seat on the first refugee train. 99 (Martindale, 1944 p154)

Rose Squire, who also wrote a detailed account of her work as a factory inspector, explained just how much the outbreak of war, arriving 'like a thief in the night' (Squire, 1927 p169), affected the work of inspectors in the Factory Department:

> 66 It came upon me as it came upon others, changing as in a moment the outlook on life, upsetting all values ... It was for the Factory Department as if a sponge had wiped off the slate all that was written there, and no one knew what to write in its place. 99 (Squire, 1927 p169)

Protective clothing: outdoor labourer's suit

Writing in the Annual Report for 1914, she commented that during the first months of the war:

❝ the encouragement the appearance of the Inspector, as usual, gave the worker, (was) often commented upon, and I believe contributed to the steadiness and cheerfulness which have been such a feature of that trying time. ❞

Reorganised production

Hilda Martindale records how in the closing months of 1914 employers diversified production, particularly into manufacturing products for which 'we had most depended on the industrial nations of Central Europe'. Leather goods, enamel ware, china, were made to different specifications, 'in fact on all sides we witnessed articles being manufactured not previously made in this country' (Martindale, 1944 p154).

The adaptability of female labour was such that she could report from the Midlands:

❝ Black Country workers had been engaged in surgical dressings factories, dressmakers and tailoresses in canvas knapsacks factories, cigar makers in electric lamp factories, fish-hook makers had become hosiery needle makers, in fact it almost seemed as if women and girls had been playing the game of general post. " (Martindale, 1944)

And then came the substitution of men by women on a scale which could scarcely be believed. Martindale observes:

" This took us all by surprise, for it must be remembered that up to 1914, what was men's work and what was women's work was far more clearly defined than it was in 1939. This happening came almost as a shock, notwithstanding that it met with the approval of some of us. " (Martindale, 1944)

Matters associated with this war-time substitution of men by women were to occupy the women inspectors for the duration of the war. There was extensive consultation with employers' organisations and trade unions, with Trade Conferences being set up 'to consider what measures might be necessary in order to free as many men as possible for the army'. (ARCI, 1915)

Rose Squire claims for the Factory Department a very special role in all the rapid changes which took place:

" Who but the men and women of the Inspectorate knew where materials were to be found, where machinery and plant suitable for mass production, where trained and disciplined staffs of workers? " (Squire, 1927 p171)

There was a massive influx of women and young workers into the production of munitions. A Ministry of Munitions was formed with Lloyd George in charge in 1915, and Rose Squire was appointed to the 'Health of Munition Workers Committee' set up in September 1915. Among her fellow appointees to this committee was May Tennant, her colleague from 20 years before, and one of

Protective clothing: light tunic suit

the first two women inspectors. The committee gave urgent attention to the difficult problem of:

" how to increase the production of munitions and equipment for our troops and at the same time preserve the health and safety of the workers and promote their physical and moral welfare. " (Squire 1927, p173)

Much attention focused upon night work and long hours of employment, but the committee also gave extensive consideration to other questions:

" The absence of facilities for feeding the vast numbers congregated in the works; the need for protection against poisoning and explosion in the manufacture of explosives or filling of shells; the supervision of young persons; arrangements for the care of the infants and little children of the hosts of married women employed. " (p174)

On the latter point, Squire records that 31 nurseries were set up by the Ministry of Munitions in addition to the 131 which began receiving maintenance grants through the Board of Education.

Reorganised inspection

Alongside the influx of women workers into industrial employment, there came an increased involvement of women in inspection. 'By 1916, 43 (male) inspectors were doing essential service elsewhere, and 45 were serving in H M Forces' (Squire, 1927 p172). Their place was taken, to some extent, by women recruited on a temporary basis: Adelaide Anderson recalls: 'the number of women inspectors gradually increased, but only to a total of thirty' (1922 p227).

They included some who were married, and Anderson later remarked: 'it was very pleasing during the war period to be told how heads of firms sometimes specially appreciated visits from married women inspectors, who were employed at that time by the Department in a temporary capacity' (Anderson, 1922 p217). In her Annual Report for 1915, Anderson commented upon the 'zealous and efficient help not only of temporary paid inspectors, but also of four unpaid' (ARCI, 1915).

Outside welfare

A curious aspect of the factory inspectors' work during World War I is described in some detail by Martindale in her memoir. This concerned their attempts to promote what was referred to as 'outside welfare'. The recruitment and substitution of women - some 1½ million entered the labour force during the war (Boston p126) - meant that many women and girls were working in unfamiliar environments, in factories and workshops where previously the workforce had been male, often some distance from their homes. The women inspectors now displayed their particular skill in understanding how conditions outside work related to those more properly called 'working conditions'. Martindale observed:

" For example, when investigating cases of toxic jaundice, it was found that the girls suffering were, owing to inconvenient train or tram service, regularly away from their homes for sixteen to eighteen hours daily; it became evident that, in spite of good conditions in the factory, the workers were bound to suffer, and that the question of transit wanted rectifying. " (Martindale, 1944 p166)

Fixing studded tread onto motor tyres

Building rubber treads for motor tyres

Stripping and hoisting tyres onto frames

Motor tyre worker

Other matters to which they gave attention included hostels, nurseries, and complaints of 'immoral conduct in factories' and of 'drinking amongst girls and women in works'; the latter to be dealt with by 'healthy forms of recreation'. (Martindale, 1944 p166)

Hilda Martindale was a member of three outside welfare committees during 1917, as well as the Birmingham Works Morality Committee. The question of drinking and drunkenness among women seems to have occupied a considerable amount of the committee members' time. Despite the imposition of a restriction order in Birmingham in 1915 (through the Central Liquor Control Board), continuing problems of drunkenness were identified and linked with female munition workers. Miss Martindale was one of three women appointed by the Control Board to investigate, under the chairmanship of Sir George Newman. She records:

❝ I visited a very large number of public houses (I think I visited over 200) at night, on Saturdays and on Sundays. It was a curious experience; we sometimes joined the frequenters of these places at their tables or at the bar, and got into conversation with them. At other times we pretended to be looking for 'Emily', and went round the licensed premises searching for her amongst the crowd. In these ways we could observe the 'drinks' which were being taken, and the results. Although the public houses were generally packed with women and girls, they were quite orderly; in fact I never found a woman drunk. Most of them had nowhere to sit, their lodgings being overcrowded, so they came to the public house. 〞 〞 (Martindale, 1944 p167)

Among the Committee's conclusions was the judgement that, although widespread, the use made of public houses by female workers did not interfere substantially or directly with the 'output of munitions'. But Martindale recalls that she 'longed to see' Winter Gardens: 'well lighted and well warmed, with plenty of comfortable seats, where the girls could come and rest and do nothing if they wished' (p167). The establishment in 1916 of a Birmingham Civic Recreation League went some way towards meeting the needs which Miss Martindale and her fellow committee members had identified.

Wartime changes in the regulation of employment

Perhaps the most important work of inspection during World War One, however, was the regulation of dangerous work, the supervision of hours of employment regulations, which were substantially modified to accommodate the war effort, and the provision of welfare facilities inside the factories.

Already in the Annual Report of the Chief Factory Inspector for 1915 it was reported that considerable 'latitude' in factory hours of employment had been allowed. During that first full year of war the Women's Branch of the Factory Inspectorate acquired special responsibility for the administration of Emergency Orders in munitions-related factories. The Principal Lady Inspector reported that her staff supplied reports and made recommendations during the year for 'over 400' munitions factories. During 1915, the Health of Munition Workers Committee was set up, and

included Rose Squire as one of its members. On the basis of factory inspectors' reports, the committee advised the Home Secretary on the issue of Emergency Orders restricting the hours of women and young persons. Squire notes that:

❝ the preliminary work of investigation, and the enforcement of the orders by day and by night, was the special work of the women's branch of the inspectorate. 〞 〞 (Squire, 1922 p175)

By 1916, the work of investigating the specially dangerous processes in which women workers were involved took much of the inspectors' time. There was particular concern about toxic jaundice among women workers, which was being observed both in the doping departments of aeroplane works and in the TNT departments of shell-filling factories. The Principal Lady Inspector remarked in the Annual Report for 1916 that this work:

Acetylene welder

Aerographing planes

Painting aircraft distinction marks

Aircraft frame making

66 had also involved much watching of experiments in progress and many consultations with workers, managers, foremen and forewomen, as to suitable protective clothing, adaptations of method, appliances and machinery, health and safety arrangements in factories, works, yards, etc. 99 (ARCI, 1916)

Hilda Martindale was inspecting in a filling factory when a serious explosion occurred. Although herself uninjured, several girl workers were hurt in this incident. She noted that especially in the early years of the war some of these incidents happened because female workers 'had taken the places of men on machines with very little instruction' (Martindale, 1944 p164). She reports that in 1916, 31 women died of toxic jaundice associated with TNT, and a further 42 in 1917, commenting:

66 It was distressing visiting some of these cases in hospital, and seeing the suffering to which the women and girls were subjected. ... between 1914 and 1918 women were called on to take their share of death and suffering to an extent which the public in no way realised. 99 (Martindale, 1944 p164)

Rose Squire also took pains to record her admiration for the women who worked in these dangerous industries:

66 The greatest peril ... was in works which were engaged in the manufacture of high explosives. Here the courage of all the women and girls was indeed remarkable. ... All submitted willingly to rigorous regulations as to dress and behaviour. From these, of course, inspectors are not exempt; indeed we set an example by readily conforming to such details as removal of hairpins (no bobbed hair then), changing into rubber shoes, etc. (Squire, 1927 p181-2)

Inspecting steel shell bars

Trucking steel shell bars

Miss Squire re-deployed

Towards the end of the war, Rose Squire's experience of this type of work led to her departure from the Factory department. The Welfare Department of the Ministry of Munitions, with which the women inspectors had been working closely since its formation, was floundering without a firm hand to steer it, and on the advice of May Tennant Miss Squire's name was put forward. Although she did not want to go, feeling her duty 'was to stay where I was', she found it impossible to resist:

66 Mr Winston Churchill, then Minister of Munitions, sent for me at the end of February (1918), and I, as well as the Home Office, fell a victim to his importunity. I am not likely to forget that long and very confidential interview which altered the course of my official life for two years and gave me the most difficult task throughout that time which I think a woman Civil Servant could endeavour to accomplish. Although, as I now believe, my absence from my own Department ... militated against the fulfilment of some of my cherished hopes of promotion, I have never regretted my decision. 99 (Squire, 1927 p179)

She never returned to the Factory Department, finding at the end of her two-year assignment that her work was still required there, in what became the Department of Demobilisation and Resettlement. Her duties, in charge now of the Women's Training Branch, included offering training programmes to women workers who were displaced at the end of the war. (McFeely, p150-1)

A broader experience of inspection

The war gave women inspectors perhaps more opportunity than ever before to investigate conditions in the whole range of industrial production. In 1917, Miss Anderson, the Principal Lady Inspector, reported that women were now employed in 'shipbuilding, steel and iron works, crane-driving and construction work.' Accidents which had occurred where cranes were in use prompted her to point out the need for improved means of access to overhead cranes and better fencing to all shafting during the traverse motions of cranes. During that same year she herself surveyed conditions in the new aircraft factories and gave advice as to methods of heating and ventilating dope rooms. (ARCI, 1917)

Significant advances were made during World War I in the provision of welfare within factories. The 1916 Police, Factories, etc (Miscellaneous Provisions) Act gave the Secretary of State new powers to enforce welfare arrangements.

Miss Martindale reports this development with some glee:

66 In future the occupiers of factories could be required to provide such amenities as mess-rooms or canteens, washing conveniences, accommodation for clothing, seats, first-aid requirements, drinking water, protective clothing and welfare supervision. This was a tremendous

Canteen dining room

step forward; now we could require the provision of seats in factories! " (Martindale, 1944 p165)

The provision of first-aid facilities was especially important during the war. Three women inspectors appointed in 1918 were recruited specifically to assist in this area. They were all women with medical backgrounds, whose role within the Women's Branch of the Inspectorate was to administer First Aid and Ambulance Orders.

The hours of employment worked by women and girls during the First World War were long. The Emergency Orders meant that both night work and extended hours could be permitted when the war effort required it. Martindale explains:

" The latitude allowed under the Orders was wide. Some factories worked their women and girl workers up to 77.5 hours per week, others worked a day and night shift of 12 hours, a few tried three shifts of 8 hours, others tried to get an increase of output by working on Sundays... (Women workers) worked at night, although such employment carried with it conditions with which they were quite unfamiliar, and in spite of the fact that sleep during the day in their little houses in noisy streets was almost an impossibility. " (Martindale, 1944 p159)

Martindale was specially interested to note as the war went on that the better organised factories reverted to shorter hours of employment, and dispensed with Sunday work. The longer the hours, she observed, the more occupiers seemed to be 'extraordinarily hazy' about factory output.

Some aspects of women workers' conditions during the war gave the women inspectors pleasure. Miss Anderson noted that in scientific instrument making the substitution of women during the war meant that 'new openings appeared for women as works' chemists or in laboratory research at the

Canteen kitchen

factory, as well as in the manufacture of glass prisms, lenses, thermometers and many metal processes'. (Anderson, 1922 p236) Her disappointment when after the war these developments were rapidly put into reverse was of course all the greater. In 1920 she reported:

66 (there is) as yet no fulfilment of the expectations that after the War a body of industries and operations offering a hopeful field of fresh employment would be open to women where their war experience could be turned to account. On the contrary, an automatically operating force has closed all these expected new avenues. 99 (Anderson, 1922 p236)

Hilda Martindale also found some developments to her liking:

66 I admit I rejoiced to see one result of this war-time work; in 1912 in Birmingham the average weekly wage for a woman working sixty hours a week in a factory was 10s to 11s. I witnessed these wages rise with almost lightning speed, and in

Canteen dining room

Canteen dining room

consequence the women provided with food which in quantity and quality was a novelty to them; but it was depressing that it required a war to show us such an elementary fact as that the stamina of the working woman depended on the nourishment she could obtain. " (Martindale, 1944 p159-60)

After the war

By the end of World War I, the importance of women's contribution both to industrial production and to the inspection and regulation of women's conditions in employment could be in no doubt. There was to be little genuine recognition of the former. Although the granting of the vote to women over 30 in 1918 is often seen as women's 'reward' for their war efforts, this would be to make too simple a connection. In fact the most striking development was the speed with which women were turned out of the jobs they had been doing, many of them returning reluctantly to domestic service. Rose Squire felt this was 'inevitable' although she was concerned about 'the hardships of unemployment' (Squire, 1927 p189). Adelaide Anderson was dismayed to find women displaced not just from their wartime employment, but also from some trades where they had traditionally

predominated: in 1920 she noted in the annual report that women were even losing some of their jobs in laundries.

For the more senior women inspectors the close of the war brought recognition in the form of official honours. In 1917 the King had created a new honour, the Most Excellent Order of the British Empire: that year, Adelaide Anderson was among the first to be appointed to the new Order when she was made a Companion of the Order (CBE), and in 1918, in the New Year's Honours, Rose Squire, Deputy Lady Inspector, was made an Officer of the Order. Hilda Martindale too was honoured:

" That year I was made an Officer of the British Empire, and it was my good fortune to be summoned to Buckingham Palace to be decorated by King George V a few days after the Armistice was declared. " (Martindale, p169)

The Women's Branch disbanded

With Rose Squire absent on secondment, and other changes in prospect, the days of the Women's Branch of the Factory Department were nearly over. Within a year of the end of the war, a committee had been established to review the structure of the Factory Department. Hilda Martindale summarises the work of the women

inspectors up to this point, and indicates her attitude to the changes which were to take place:

" From the first, the women were granted equal powers with their men colleagues as far as women's trades were concerned; they worked under their own women officers; they formed their own

Rounding off corners at a saw mill

Machine wiring at a saw mill

standard of inspection. Except in certain trades, however, they referred technical matters in connection with machinery to their men colleagues. Also, they were not given certain of the responsibilities of the District Inspectors, for example the keeping of records and the regular visiting of workplaces. Then came the war. ... Their duties were extended, they gained more knowledge and experience in technical questions, and an entry to those factories which had hitherto been inspected only by men. ... It was obvious that some change in the organisation was necessary. ...

The Chief Inspector was strongly in favour of giving the women still more responsibility with the definite status of District Inspector and Superintending Inspector. Mr Asquith stated in the House that as regards the great professions and particularly the Services of the State, women ought to be placed on precise equality with men. "
(Martindale, 1944 p172-3)

A relatively recent appointee to the Women's Branch, Miss Constance Smith, now came to prominence in the planning and implementation of

Tongue and grooving

changes affecting women inspectors. Throughout the war, having joined the staff as a senior woman inspector in 1913, Miss Smith had been an important member of the women staff. She already had substantial experience of women's employment issues as a volunteer, and had been active in the Women's Trade Union League. She was also, as McFeely points out (p123), a founder member of the International Association for Labour Legislation, the forerunner of the International Labour Organisation. She was already in her fifties when recruited.

Perhaps because she was a later recruit to the Women's Branch, she was an important ally for the Chief Inspector of Factories, Sir Malcolm Delevingne, who now wanted to form an integrated organisation, and to disband the Women's Branch. (McFeely, 1988 p154)

The Principal Lady Inspector, Adelaide Anderson CBE, was appointed to the small committee looking into reorganisation. McFeely reports in some detail the deep disappointment which the reorganisation plan, when it was finally agreed, represented for Adelaide Anderson. It is obvious that she would to some extent see the changes proposed as undermining 20 years of work. Anderson's own

proposals for change amounted to little more than retention of the status quo, with improved communications. Miss Smith could not agree; and she wrote confidentially to her friend Violet Markham:

66 this attempt to wrap women ... in silver paper, and to provide them with a chaperon in the person of the Senior Lady Inspector (would) keep the women inspectors in a side current. 99 (quoted in McFeely, 1988 p156)

She believed this would be wrong, and that it would make for difficulties in recruiting able women.

Miss Martindale found herself able to accept the reorganisation plan which was eventually agreed 'although I was not altogether in favour of the scheme' (Martindale, 1944 p175). For her, there was sugar on the pill: for when the decision to abolish the posts formerly held by women was announced, with women 'regarded as eligible for all posts', it was also announced that a number of senior posts would be reserved for women. There would be posts for women as Deputy Chief Inspector (1); as Superintending

Tin plate worker

Punching fish plates onto steel rails

Hack saw operators

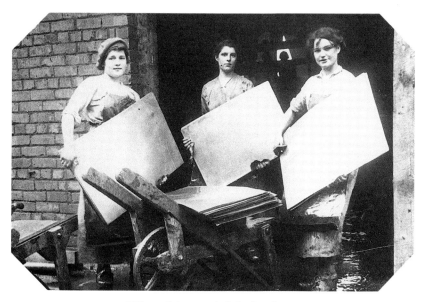

Trucking pickled plates

Inspectors (2) and as District Inspectors (8). The Annual Report of the Chief Inspector for 1920 also makes clear that:

66 Women Divisional and District Inspectors will also be appointed. ... In Divisions under a man Superintending Inspector a woman will be appointed as an additional Deputy Superintending Inspector ... she will have special duties in regard to the women's work in the Division, and special arrangements will be made to keep her in touch with the women Inspectors. ... Men junior inspectors may be attached to districts under women District inspectors and vice versa. 99 (ARCI, 1920)

Miss Martindale records her personal reaction:

66 I learned that I was to be the Superintending Inspector for the Southern Division; thus I was no longer a lady inspector! 99 (Martindale, 1944 p174)

She had two main concerns about the changes: that she 'should have to face the prejudice and somewhat natural opposition of the men Inspectors' (p175) and that 'the women Inspectors would find themselves handicapped by

Opening tin plates

their inferior technical knowledge, as only a few women had graduated in engineering subjects in those days' (p175). She found her first concerns 'were not groundless' - one older male colleague commented to her 'I am in the horrible position of having to work under a woman - yourself' and although things 'settled down':

66 the position was not easy, and many times from then onwards I envied men being able to get on with their work without having to contend with sex prejudice. 99 (p175)

Miss Anderson's retirement

While Miss Martindale's new position gave her new opportunities, there was intense disappointment for Adelaide Anderson. Not only was her post as Principal Lady Inspector abolished, but no place was found for her in the new arrangements. It was decided at senior level that she should retire, although she was only 57. The decision was relayed to her belatedly, and unexpectedly: she was shocked and dismayed as were many of her women colleagues. Rose Squire was among the many who wrote heartfelt letters (below).

To add insult to injury, the bare three month's notice, at the age of 57, meant a reduced pension because she had 'retired' early. She was made a Dame of the British Empire in recognition of her

> 23 Clifton Hill NW8
> May 18th 1921
>
> My dearest Adelaide
>
> In the first few days of these happenings which have turned our world upside down and stunned us, I felt unable to write to you but now I feel impelled to try and write (speech is impossible one breaks down!) what however I am at a loss to express of the love, gratitude, admiration and honour which I have for you and in which I hold you. ...
>
> To how few is it given as in your case to occupy an absolutely unique position, never has anyone before been Principal Lady Inspector of Factories (and all that the office has meant) and never again will anyone be that. ...
>
> With much love and all best wishes
>
> Yours affectionately
>
> Rose Squire

Adelaide Anderson's papers

Adelaide Anderson with Chinese delegation

achievements, but Sir Malcolm Delevingne was well aware that her treatment had been unfortunate. In a note to Violet Markham, he wrote:

   ❝ she gets hardly three months' notice. If you or Mrs Tennant can pour any balm it will be a work of charity. I wish she could be put in the way of some work, either official or other, but nothing has suggested itself so far. ❞ (quoted in McFeely, 1988 p160-1)

Characteristically, Adelaide Anderson accepted her honour, and her retirement, the latter under protest. She was soon using her new status to good effect in her overseas work, most notably in China where she gave advice on industrial conditions. Her work there was appreciated, and she wrote about it in her book, *Humanity and labour in China* (1928).

Rose Squire was disappointed too. Although on secondment outside the Factory Department, as Miss Anderson's deputy she might have expected the post of Deputy Chief Inspector. It was not offered to her. She remained in the Department of Demobilisation and Resettlement, and the post of Deputy Chief Inspector went instead to Constance Smith, who was capable and known to support the amalgamation arrangements. Miss Squire is recorded in the Annual Report for 1921, like Dame Adelaide Anderson, as having 'retired'.

Although Miss Smith now took over as senior woman (until her retirement in 1925), and deserves credit for the smoothness with which, in all the circumstances, the reorganisation of the Department took place, it was soon to be Miss Martindale's turn to take prominence.

Miss Constance Smith, OBE, HM Deputy Chief Inspector of Factories 1921-1925

Miss Martindale and developments after World War I

Miss Martindale, as Deputy Chief Inspector from 1925 to 1933, left her mark both in particular areas of factory inspection work, especially safety promotion, and in the organisation of the Department.

The Safety First Movement emerged after the war, with women inspectors' involvement regularly noted in the Annual Reports. Miss Martindale notes that:

66 Safety Committees in factories were established to carry out regular inspections of the machinery and plant, and it was being realised that there was a psychological side to accident prevention which should not be neglected. This was brought home to me when investigating an accident which had happened to a girl working on a platen machine resulting in the loss of her left hand. She had been employed on this machine for five years, and it was guarded in accordance with the standard of those days. When I visited her in hospital I learned she had recently lost her mother, that her father was out of work and that she had been going through a period of great emotional strain. It was impossible not to feel that a discerning foreman or forewoman would have transferred her to a less dangerous machine for a time. First-Aid arrangements in factories were being rapidly introduced during these years and in this way we tried to lessen the serious consequences of accidents. 99 (Martindale, 1944 p176)

There was also increasing attention to matters such as lighting in factories, lifting (especially by women and young persons - in 1925 the first woman to be appointed as a Medical Inspector of Factories contributed a report on this subject), and welfare, particularly involving women in the case of herring curing. Two aspects of Miss Martindale's work in these years are of special interest: her involvement with the Home Office Industrial Museum; and her role, on becoming the senior Deputy Chief Inspector, with respect to staffing issues.

The Home Office Industrial Museum

Although the Industrial Museum had been planned before the First World War, and a building constructed to house it in 1913, it was not until 1925 that it could be properly established. This date coincided with Miss Martindale's promotion from Superintending Inspector to Deputy Chief Inspector, and provided her with the opportunity to become closely involved with its development. Among her new duties - which included receiving for the necessary action 'all the papers in regard to employment, sanitation, truck, particulars, welfare and the Potteries' (Martindale, 1944 p177) - was that of responsibility for the organisation of the museum. She saw this as 'a unique opportunity to see

Rubber machine operator

Calandering sheet rubber

Vulcanising rubber tubes

some of my dreams become realities'. (p177)

The development of the exhibitions was overseen by Miss Martindale and a 'small committee of technical inspectors', together with the Chief Inspector. She herself took responsibility for the laundry and welfare exhibits.

The museum was opened on 5 December 1927. Miss Martindale reports with pride the preliminary visit made by the King and Queen, during which 'I had the honour of showing Queen Mary some industrial exhibits' and the visit a few months later of the Duke and Duchess of York 'who had concerned themselves to such a marked degree with the problems of safety, health and welfare in industry' a few months later (29 Feb 1928). Besides being open to the public, and used by employers, managers, supervisory staff and workers, the museum was also used for training of inspectors, and as a place where refresher courses were run.

This work also took her abroad: in 1920 she attended a Conference of Directors of Industrial Safety Museums, at the invitation of the German Government. This was held in Berlin, at the Deutschen Arbeitz Schutz-Museum, Charlottenberg, under the auspices of the International Labour Organisation. Along with the Dutch director, Hilda Martindale was appointed a Deputy Chairman of the Conference. The Conference resolved to meet again, in 1931, 'at the invitation of Great Britain at the Home Office Industrial Museum' (ARCI, 1929 p71).

In following years, other women inspectors became closely associated with the museum, Miss Crundwell, Miss Dingle and Miss Taylor being especially mentioned in the reports.

Staffing issues

The reorganisation of 1921-22 had marked a major change in the way that the women factory inspectors worked, and as such it was appropriate that it should be reviewed after several years. Miss Martindale, with her special responsibility for staffing issues, was well aware that although 'integration' had been achieved, there were some outstanding anomalies. These she described as:

" separate recruitment for men and women, separate seniority lists, and a few special posts for women, which ... had not been satisfactory. "

In 1928 a six-member departmental committee was established under the chairmanship of Sir Vivian Henderson (Parliamentary Under-Secretary, Home Office), with Miss Martindale as one of its two women members, to review the reorganisation which had been put into effect in 1921.

When the committee reported in 1930 it had held 20 meetings and examined 32 witnesses, as well as '19 members of various grades and sections of the Inspectorate' (Report, 1930). The report included brief comment on the history of the Women's Branch, and the following table indicating 'the present establishment'.

Chief Inspector	1
Deputy Chief Inspector (1 woman)	3
Medical Inspectors (1 woman)	5
Electrical Inspectors	5
Engineering Inspectors	6
Inspectors of Textile Particulars	5
Total Headquarters and technical staff	25
Superintending Inspectors (1 woman)	10
Deputy Superintending Inspectors (1 woman; 9 Class 1A)	10
Woman Deputy Superintending Inspectors	6
Other Inspectors - Class 1A	18
Inspectors - Class 1B	58
Woman District Inspectors	8
Inspectors - Class II	35
Woman Inspectors	16
Inspectors' Assisstants	19
Total Divisional and District Staff	180
Total Staff	205

Trucking raw rubber

The report noted that this establishment represented an increase in the headquarters and technical staff (from 19 to 25 since 1914) but a decrease, effectively of 17 posts, to 190 posts at divisional and district level. This reduction had coincided with a marked increase in duties: new work arose from new codes of regulations for dangerous and unhealthy industries; from the introduction of Welfare Orders, from the Women and Young Persons (Employment in Lead Processes) Act 1920, from the Employment of Women, Young Persons and Children Act, 1920, from the Workmen's Compensation Act, 1923, and from the Lead Paint (Protection against Poisoning) Act of 1926, as well as by more general expansion of the Inspectorate's work in promoting health and safety.

Of considerable interest for the future employment of women inspectors were the committee's conclusions about the deployment of male and female inspectors. The committee had considered 'detailed' proposals for re-allocating men and women staff to particular types of work on the basis of sex:

66 The general idea of this scheme was to make the men inspectors responsible for the inspection of machinery and the handling of safety questions generally, and to assign to the women inspectors the sphere of welfare. Apart from other considerations, we felt it was far too complicated to work well in practice. ... The present organisation has been in operation for nearly 8 years and no suggestion has been made from any quarter that the work of inspection is not being carried on efficiently. 99

Other proposals were put forward to extend the scheme under which 'works in the heavy industries are generally left to the men inspectors' (Home Office Report, 1930, p24). Employers' representatives had:

66 referred to the absence among the women inspectors of technical engineering qualifications

Doping glasses for anti-gas masks

Varnishing glasses for anti-gas masks

Packing anti-gas masks

and an alleged inability to sense the 'works atmosphere', but the point upon which they laid most stress was that the inspection of these works by women inspectors was not acceptable to the employers and that this 'lack of acceptance' must militate against the results achieved by the women inspectors. We have no evidence however to show that this apprehension has been borne out by actual experience and the employers' representatives did not advance any cases in which the women inspectors had in any way failed in the duties placed upon them since 1921. On the contrary, it was admitted that the women inspectors did not miss anything in their inspections and the evidence as a whole shows that they have carried out their work with efficiency and zeal. Moreover, the representatives of the Trades Union Congress General Council expressed the view that women inspectors were fully as competent as the men and told us that they did not see any objection at all to women inspectors dealing with works where only men are employed.

We understand that the view put forward by the employers' representatives is chiefly based on psychological grounds of a rather vague nature, and we do not feel we should be justified in making it the basis of a recommendation involving a serious departure from the existing system. We anticipate that, as inspection by the women inspectors develops, any sentiment of opposition to inspection by women as such, will tend to disappear. 🙶🙶 (Home Office Report, 1930 p24)

Who, reading these lines, can fail to hear Miss Martindale's voice and acerbic comment as she contributed to the discussions on this topic? Indeed, Miss Martindale and her fellow committee members came to the conclusion, not just that such regressive proposals vis-a-vis women inspectors should be rejected, but that their place in the Inspectorate should be strengthened:

66 The present proportion of women in the divisional and district staff is 18 per cent. We have no hesitation in saying that this proportion is too small ... We recommend that this proportion should be increased within the next few years to 30 per cent. 99

The committee nevertheless held out against complete 'fusion', rejecting the idea that 'all promotions' should be made on the basis of common seniority on the grounds that:

66 the time has not yet come when complete fusion can be adopted. We consider it important in the interests of the Service that inspectors of each sex should hold a certain number of higher posts and it is clear that under present conditions this can only be secured in the case of women by special arrangements. 99

The decision to both enlarge the staff of the Inspectorate and to increase the proportion of women to a target figure of 30 per cent was one which clearly

pleased Hilda Martindale. She was soon off on a 'recruiting campaign' visiting 'practically every University in the country' to explain the Department's needs, and to encourage suitable candidates, both male and female, to come forward. From then on, she noted:

66 Men and women were interviewed by the same (Selection) Board and were arranged in order of merit, and it was very cheering for me the first time a woman was put at the head of that list. 99 (Martindale, 1944 p186)

Still feeling that women were 'to a certain degree handicapped by their want of mechanical knowledge' she went further: she visited Loughborough College of Engineering and met with its Principal, Professor Schofield, who agreed to:

66 arrange a simplified course of engineering for women. This course proved a great success and has given to women some of the knowledge familiar to most men. 99 (Martindale, 1944 p186)

Among the women who attended it were Miss Norah Curry and Miss Cecily Tabb, whose careers as factory inspectors are referred to in the following chapter.

International activities

In 1931 and again in 1932 Hilda Martindale represented the Factory Department as technical adviser on questions associated with the employment of women and children at the 15th Session of the International Labour Conference, held in Geneva. Constance Smith had earlier chaired sessions on women's employment at the 1919 meeting of the ILO held in Washington DC. These

conferences were 'not to be missed'. There was a large British delegation, and 47 nations were represented.

66 The number of women attending as delegates or representatives was, alas, small, but I enjoyed the opportunity of meeting those from other lands. 99

LOUGHBOROUGH COLLEGE

Special Training Course
in Simplified Engineering for Women

having in view employment as

FACTORY INSPECTORS, WELFARE SUPERVISORS,
and ADMINISTRATIVE and MANAGERIAL
ASSISTANTS IN INDUSTRY

Loughborough college prospectus, front cover

Special Training Course in Simplified Engineering

THERE is an increasing demand for trained women who have had some practical experience of engineering, and who are familiar with the conditions in Industrial Workshops, to occupy positions as Factory Inspectors, Welfare Supervisors, Secretaries to Engineers, or obtain Managerial Posts, etc.

To meet this demand a short course of training has therefore been arranged for women who are sufficiently qualified in other directions to gain experience of engineering processes in the Workshops of the College.

The normal course will occupy at least twelve weeks, of which six will be spent in works, where the students will be required to do actual work, so that they may become acquainted with the various tools and processes.

Those taking the Course will be withdrawn from the Shops to take the ordinary College lectures on Workshop Processes. These lectures will occupy about three hours per week.

Whilst in the Works students will be required to comply with the normal workshop regulations, to keep the workshop hours, and to " clock in " to register their attendance.

It will be appreciated that this course cannot in any sense be regarded as a training in engineering proper, but is intended to give women employed in industry a working knowledge of machinery and engineering processes and terminology.

Page Three

Loughborough college prospectus, introductory page

Her brief in 1931 was to advise on the night employment of women. Although she was a strong believer in protective legislation for women, she took on the role at this and a subsequent ILO Conference of proposing an amendment to the ILO Convention (which Britain had implemented in its 1920 Employment of Women, Young Persons and Children Act) prohibiting women's night work. Her aim was to enable professional women to be exempted. A case had arisen following the Women's Engineering Society's successful bid to gain for women a share in rural electrification, in which two women had been illegally employed as managers of country power stations in Devon. The British Government felt such employment, although comprising night work, should be available to women. Miss Martindale recounts her role in proposing and speaking to the amendment in her memoir. This involved two attempts, in 1932 and later in 1934 after she had left the Factory Department, with the result:

66 that women holding managerial posts would not in future be precluded from carrying on their duties at night. This has been implemented in Section 79 of the Factories Act, 1937. 99 (Martindale, 1944 p183)

Miss Martindale transferred to Treasury

By 1933 Miss Martindale had given more than thirty years' service as a factory inspector, reaching the most senior rank realistically available to women when she was appointed a Deputy Chief Inspector in 1922. Now a further promotion was to take her out of the Factory Department. In early 1933 Dame Maude Lawrence, Director of Women Establishments at HM Treasury, died, leaving vacant the post which was 'regarded as the highest post for women in the Civil Service'. Hilda Martindale was invited to apply for the position, but declined to do so as she 'was not in favour of special posts for women of this nature'. (1944 p188) She was nevertheless summoned to appear before the Selection Board, and given the appointment. She left the Factory Department reluctantly, but confident of her successor's abilities:

66 Fortunately my colleague, Miss Taylor, was well qualified to take my place, a post she has held with great acumen for the last ten years.

... During my seven years as a Deputy Chief Inspector, the number of women inspectors had been more than doubled and I knew I was leaving in the Factory Department ... a splendid staff of younger women well trained to carry on the traditions of the past with a fresh outlook on the problems before them. 99   (1944 p189)

Indeed there had been substantial intakes of new women inspectors in the 1920s and early 1930s: they included women who were themselves to become prominent inspectors: Miss D Johnson and Miss F E Messiter, appointed in 1922; Miss K Crundwell, appointed 1926; Miss V Chinn and Miss A S Bettenson, appointed in 1930; Miss E K Blackburn, appointed 1931. Of these, Miss Vera Chinn is the sole survivor in 1992. She very generously gave a detailed interview to the present author, and in that way has made a special contribution to the account of the years between 1930 and 1960.

Recollections of World War II

While the activities of women factory inspectors in World War I are recorded in some detail in the annual reports of the Chief Inspector of Factories and in the memoirs of individual inspectors, women's role in factory inspection in World War II is more difficult to identify. Annual reporting during this period was very limited, and the sex of inspectors is rarely mentioned. Many women were recruited as temporary inspectors during the war, and those who were already in place continued in post. The most senior woman during the war was Miss F I Taylor who died in 1947 leaving no detailed account of her work. However, some of those women who worked as inspectors in wartime have been interviewed for this book, while other retired inspectors have recorded their memories of wartime work in a collection compiled by Cecily Tabb and Katharine Malins Smith (1985).

Factory inspection at the outbreak of World War II

Reviewing the work of the Factory Department in 1939, the Chief Inspector noted that, like that of the whole country, it had 'been overshadowed by the outbreak of war in 1939' (ARCI, 1939 p1). One effect of wartime conditions, he reported, was to hold back the encouraging developments which he was confident he would otherwise have been in a position to record. For the implementation of the Factory Act, 1937, from July 1938 onwards had only just begun:

66 Occupiers of factories were falling into line and something like a new order in working conditions was being inaugurated. 99 (ARCI, 1939)

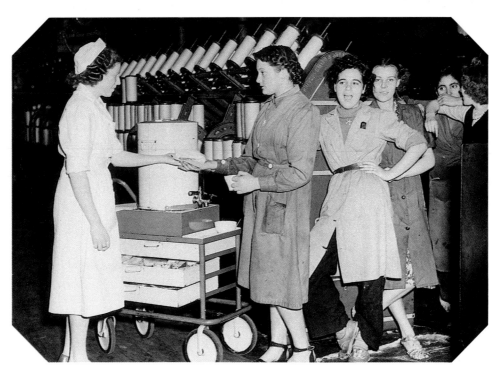

World War II canteen facilities

There were, however, new developments affecting factory inspectors to report. These included work under the Civil Defence Act 1939 'in relation to the provision of shelter against air attack' of factories. This work had begun in April 1939, and the Minister of Home Security had reported in Parliament on the 'invaluable service' which factory inspectors had done. Their responsibilities included ensuring that air raid shelters were provided in factories, and that factory personnel were trained and equipped to respond appropriately when air raids took place.

On the negative side, a marked increase in accidents had to be reported following the outbreak of war: in the case of fatal accidents, the increase had been of 42% (comparing Sept 1939 - Feb 1940 with Sept 1938 - Feb 1939). The Chief Inspector noted:

❝ In spite of warnings by the Government, little effort was made to black-out our factories up to this time (September 1939), and as a consequence many fatalities occurred in the rush to get this black-out work done. The number of fatalities for this month (129) is the highest of which I can find record. ❞ (ARCI, 1939 p3)

Factory inspectors, he noted, needed to be particularly vigilant about accident prevention in circumstances where hours of employment would be extended, where there would be a rapid influx of new workers, and where persons were working under conditions of war-time stress.

There had been marked changes in hours of employment with the outbreak of war. The Chief Inspector reported with some dismay in 1941:

❝ Experience of the year 1940 has shown that some valuable lessons of the last war had been widely forgotten. I have particularly in mind the lessons that excessive hours mean less production and that proper breaks and rest days are of great importance from the production point of view. ❞ (ARCI, 1940)

Variation in the hours of work permitted under Factory Act legislation could be arranged, as in World War I, through the Factory Department which had powers to issue Emergency Orders. Factory inspectors working throughout the war would find that dealing with arrangements under such Emergency Orders took up a good deal of their time.

recruited as a temporary inspector in about 1944, and sent to work in Leicester:

66 The man who was in charge was meant to be training her. He intended to take her out to investigate an accident, so they went out together in his car, and he said, 'Well now, we'll just look at this report before we go in.' So they looked at this report, and he said, 'What we shall have to do is this, this and this'. So she said, 'OK.' And then he said, 'Well, I've told you it all - why shouldn't you do it? You get on and do it. Goodbye.' Pushed her out the car and drove away! That was his method of training! 99 (interview with Norah Curry, 1992)

Others recalled being fortunate in getting helpful training from their seniors, but the normal arrangements, for example the training lectures which probationary inspectors normally attended at the Home Office Industrial Museum, were suspended for part of the war although in 1942 some training was provided by a 'short course at the Industrial Museum' (ARCI, 1942 p24). The museum itself was closed to normal visitors, and Miss Beatrice Moorcroft (recruited in 1938) recalled that her intake took their qualifying examination (arranged outside London, to avoid bringing a whole group of inspectors together in London at one time when there might be air raids) without attending such lectures. (Tabb and Malins Smith p91)

Temporary inspectors

The war necessitated the employment of temporary inspectors of factories because of a general increase in the work, additional special duties, and the diversion of some male labour from the Inspectorate into military service and other essential war work. In 1940 the Chief Inspector reported that 70 temporary inspectors had been added to the Inspectorate: a further 39 were added in 1941, and by 1945 there was a temporary staff of 130. Many of these were women.

It is no longer possible to identify all of them, since their names were not listed in the Annual Report and many left after the war. But some of these women went on to make careers in the Inspectorate, and their wartime recollections indicate the difficult work which they undertook, and the resourcefulness, courage and dedication with which they carried it out.

Many of these women were from the middle class and were university graduates; some, like Vera

Chinn and Bessie Blackburn, came from humbler backgrounds and had benefited from educational opportunities only available to the exceptionally gifted. Miss Chinn had been educated at the London School of Economics on a Mary Macarthur scholarship in the early 1920s, and Bessie Blackburn had studied on a bursary at Woodbrooke (the Quaker college) and in 1928-9 had been the Hodson Platt Memorial scholar at the Co-operative College in Manchester.

Among the graduate women, several came from Girton College, Cambridge, which decades before was where Adelaide Anderson had also studied. There, Miss Campbell, who acted as a careers adviser to graduating women, advised many of the able women who subsequently joined the Factory Inspectorate and assisted them with finding suitable employment where they might gain relevant industrial experience.

Miss Norah Curry, one of the old Girtonians who took advantage of such advice from Miss Campbell recalled that when she finished reading history in 1938:

> " She sent me to see Miss F I Taylor who was the Deputy Chief in charge of staff, and she coldly said to me, 'you have no industrial experience. You must get some if you want to join the Inspectorate'. And she recommended that I should go to Loughborough where the Engineering College was running a three-month course for women who wanted to get some knowledge of the basics of engineering. "

Following this, she worked as an unpaid volunteer in the welfare department at Churchman's tobacco factory in Ipswich, and subsequently as an unskilled employee at Standard Telephone and Cables in north London, also arranged by Miss Campbell. There she gained an insight into:

> " the view of the ordinary unskilled work person about factory life. I was putting two little bits of rubber in a metal armature with a foot press. "
> (interview with Norah Curry, 1992)

In due course the war started, and Miss Curry found herself unemployed. Miss Campbell again helped her: first finding her work as a clerical officer in the Ministry of Supply, and then as a welfare officer in an India rubber factory. After a year in this post, ' I heard that the Inspectorate were recruiting'. She was interviewed - with Miss F I Taylor on the interviewing panel - and recruited, to begin work in Norwich under the supervision of the formidable Miss F E Messiter, who was the District Inspector and had been in the Inspectorate since 1919.

Other old Girtonians who also found their way into factory inspecting, some starting before the war,

included Betty Hoyles, Katharine Malins Smith, Marion Massey, Alice Crosthwaite and Janet Moss.

Another woman who was recruited as a temporary inspector during the war was Marianne Woolgar. She was appointed in 1943, having commenced war work in Royal Ordnance Factories where she worked first as a chemist and later as Women's Labour Manager. She had a first class degree in chemistry from Birmingham University, and had subsequently been awarded her PhD there in 1934. She had married and had two children, but was widowed in 1941 when her husband, a nightfighter pilot, was killed. She entered the Inspectorate while a young mother (her children were aged six and seven years), a remarkable situation at that time. Like other women who entered the Inspectorate, Dr Woolgar felt strongly motivated to do work which would contribute to improving the working conditions of working people. She notes:

> " From the age of nine, my paternal grandfather, an ardent admirer of Keir Hardie, made sure that we knew about social conditions at the end of the 19th century and in the aftermath of the industrial revolution. "

She remembers that in Kirkheaton church graveyard:

> " there's a monument I used to look at as a child, and it's a monument to 17 children that were burnt to death in a factory fire in 1815. And I couldn't believe the children - 9, 10, 11, you know - and this used to worry me. " (interview with Marianne Wolgar, 1992)

It had been 'an easy step to the Factory Department' from such a background.

Those who were already inspectors at the outbreak of war recall how the changed circumstances affected them at first. Bessie Blackburn has written about the challenge which working in wartime presented for her deeply held Quaker beliefs. She also notes that the first change in duties was that 'I found myself in ARP work and fire-watching' (Blackburn, no date p39). Esther Harries (nee Holmes) has observed:

66 The changeover to wartime production seemed slow until after Dunkirk; then suddenly all was frenzy, and for the first time the law-abiding occupiers and workpeople of Coventry ceased to be interested in co-operating with the Inspectorate, and were only intent on getting production by means legal or illegal. This phase only lasted a few weeks, after which Ernest Bevin and Co began to take hold, and some kind of order was restored. 99 (Tabb and Malins Smith, p79)

Vera Chinn was in Ashton-under-Lyme as Divisional Inspector at the start of the war:

66 We had shelters to look out for and get provided, and other precautions. (Working at night)

I remember being terrified the Home Guard would shoot me instead of the Germans! Driving a car in the middle of Glossop in the middle of the night - at blackout! Before I knew where I was, I'd not only got a junior, but I'd got somebody doing air raid shelter, and the other protections... in a tiny little office - two rooms in Ashton-under-Lyme, one with a clerk and shorthand typist, and the other with the three of us trying to do different aspects of our work. But we did it somehow. ... It was very hard going, you know. 99 (interview with Vera Chinn, 1992)

Meanwhile the Chief Inspector was recording some of the experiences which factory inspectors had reported to him. Among these he included:

A riotous scene of a shop full of women and girls giving practically full output from automatic machines in a roofless shop, working in heavy rain in mackintoshes under the protection of a few tarpaulins, to a full chorus of "It ain't gonna rain no more." (ARCI, 1940 p6)

The large influx of female labour into factory work was to be a crucial aspect of the inspectors' wartime work.

Night inspection

As welfare developments got under way, and canteen advisers were appointed, many of the women inspectors began to do their night inspection work in the company of the local canteen adviser. This was partly because canteen advisers had no right of entry to premises, as factory inspectors did, partly to save precious fuel during petrol rationing, and partly for company in what must have been frightening work in the dead of night. Miss Chinn recalls going out inspecting at night with Mabel

Berry, who was a canteen adviser:

66 We had some adventures, as you can imagine, going out at night to the canteens. Mabel Berry was blind as a bat - I was terrified of driving with her. You had a tin thing over your headlights, with a little slit - it threw a bit of light where you were. Awful, terrible. 99 (interview with Vera Chinn)

Meanwhile Norah Curry was experiencing similar problems in East Anglia. She was allowed to drive a car, although she had been in the department a very short time, because the District Inspector, Miss Messiter, did not herself drive. The car was 'an ancient Hillman' which she purchased from her father in 1941. This meant taking her senior on many trips, which formed part of Miss Curry's training. Miss Messiter was a formidable character, and Norah Curry explains:

66 I drove her about the countryside. In blackout! I remember one time, going to a sugar beet factory right at the west end of Norfolk, and we were there until about 6. ...I (had) to drive back to Norwich, with only the standard slit headlights, and of course Miss Messiter sat beside me sleeping sweetly most of the time, and occasionally saying, 'Why do you keep driving into pub yards?' And I said 'Because you can't see them!' You know, if you're following the hedge, and it goes in, you just had to go with it. 99 (interview with Norah Curry, 1992)

Bomb damage

Other women inspectors recalled the terrible conditions during bomb raids and how these affected their work. Esther Harries was slightly injured during an early bombing raid, and then experienced the blitz while working as an inspector in Coventry. After the all-clear blew, and she had slept through sheer exhaustion for a few hours, she recalls:

66 It then came to me that, as I was the only Inspector who lived in the city, I had better see what had happened to the office. So I took a tin hat which I had irregularly acquired and set out to walk the half-mile to Greyfriars Lane. 99 (Tabbs and Malins Smith p79)

She found fires and explosions everywhere: the office had suffered a good deal of fire damage and no longer had a roof. Shortly afterwards they moved to new premises in Leamington, and as they did so, many firms were moving out of the city also. Yet she recalls:

66 Some inspection was possible, and on the days I did spend in the city the main problem was getting anything to eat. 99 (p80)

Factory conditions

Katharine Malins Smith was working in Preston in the early part of the war. She recalled the 'appalling' conditions which often resulted from the hasty black-out arrangements whereby windows were simply painted black, and had to remain shut during the hours of darkness.

66 One of our first wartime jobs was to visit, during the night, every bakehouse where night baking was carried on, to check the temperature and ventilation and to give advice about the

construction of louvres and baffles which would let in some air without letting out any light. " (Tabb and Malins Smith)

She also remembered how the situation changed in the early months of the war:

" During the crisis months of 1940 many factories were working flat out and all attempts to control hours of work were abandoned. When it began to appear that invasion was not after all imminent and that the war might last some years, it became clear that production would not be helped by exhausted workers carrying on working excessively long hours and we began to try to limit hours of work again. The Fylde was by then crowded with RAF camps. All the local laundries were inundated with RAF washing, and we issued emergency orders to allow them to work outside legal limits. In practice, this was not an exercise in allowing longer hours, but in reducing the hours they had been working to something acceptable. I remember the sense of triumph with which I succeeded, after long discussion, in persuading one laundry to agree to limit the women's hours to 60 a week. " (ibid)

Miss Curry worked during part of the war in Leicester alongside her more experienced colleague Miss Alice Ewart:

" When Miss Ewart was in a factory you always tried to get as far away as you could from her, because she was always very outspoken about this, that and the other: 'And WHY is this!', and 'WHAT is that?' I was always cringing in the background. At that time women were first starting to be employed in big proportions in the engineering works at night. They had converted boot and shoe factories into engineering works for the war, and the proportion of women in these engineering works was much higher than they had been in the boot and shoe. So that washing facilities and sanitary accommodation were very often quite inadequate in numbers. And they had the blackout, which they achieved by painting all the windows black, so you couldn't open them. So in the summer there were horrible problems of ventilation. Really there were poor conditions, so it was no wonder she got irate. " (interview with Norah Curry, 1992)

Accidents and accident prevention work

" The outstanding feature of the year, and one that has necessarily influenced the work of the Inspectorate, has been the growing importance of the work of women in factories. (...) this year the inspectors feel that women not only again increased in numbers but had a much more widely recognised position in the industrial structure of the country. " (ARCI, 1942 p3)

reported the Chief Inspector in 1942.

Many of these women were working in conditions which left a great deal to be desired. They were often employed on work for which they had received inadequate training; they were working in overcrowded and poorly ventilated premises; and they were suffering many accidents. In 1942, adult women suffered 71 244 reportable accidents, about a third of which occurred in machine making. This represented an increase of 389% on the figure for accidents to women in 1938. The Chief Inspector noted:

66 Inspectors are agreed that, apart from the increase in the numbers employed, the increase in the number of accidents to women is mainly due to the fact that women have so largely taken over those accident producing occupations formerly reserved for male workers of some skill. Last year I mentioned ... that women were safe workers when employed in jobs within their physical capacities but that they are to some extent more liable to accidents due to the catching of hair and clothing in moving machinery. 99

He went on to point out that the Factory Department remained of the opinion that 'efficient fencing' was the 'first line of defence' against such accidents, and that the wearing of caps was no guarantee of preventing hair entanglement accidents. Other common ways in which women became injured on moving machinery included the wearing of protective gloves - 'the presence of an old silk stocking on the right hand made an accident on a milling cutter so severe as to lead to amputation'. Short sleeves and no gloves or bandages were recommended, with the comment: 'work on machinery with rapidly rotating parts and the preservation of well manicured hands are incompatible'. (ARCI, 1942 p6-7)

Miss Messiter, who was a District Inspector during the war, was known for her enthusiasm for 'secure fencing'. Miss Curry recalls the poor conditions which prevailed in many wartime factories, and Miss Messiter's work:

66 I can still remember going to one factory and the lighting was little pools of light and then great stretches of darkness all around. The conditions

were very poor. ... The machinery all arrived with guarding of a poor standard, and there were a lot of accidents, and it really was very basic inspection. 99 (interview with Norah Curry 1992)

Miss Curry's initial training with Miss Messiter was particularly useful in these circumstances.

66 Miss Messiter ... was passionately interested in machinery, and how it worked, and how you should guard it. And when she took me out for a visit for instruction... she would spend hours discussing with works managers how machines should be guarded and what the guarding should be like, and whether when new machines arrived they were adequately guarded. The works manager then used to retire and say 'Excuse me, I must go and have my lunch - I'll send my deputy.' And then we would go on regardless, then the deputy would say, 'Wouldn't you like a break for a cup of tea?', and Miss Messiter would say, 'CERTAINLY NOT. Perhaps SHE might like something', indicating me. But she was absolutely devoted to improving the standard of guarding machines. ... She produced a famous booklet on what were called the unfenced machinery regulations, which were an abstruse section of the Act, which said what you should do when it was necessary to remove the guarding for some purpose. And this was her claim to fame in the Inspectorate. 99 (interview with Norah Curry, 1992)

Investigation of accidents during the war could be difficult. As Miss Cecily Tabb, who worked as an inspector in London during the war, points out:

66 It was particularly difficult during the blitz, because the person who had had the accident, if

he couldn't work, went away from London to have a rest from the raids. 🙶 (interview with Cecily Tabb, 1992)

Miss Beatrice Moorcroft, who was also a young inspector in London during the war, remembers going out with her Pocket Register (of factories and workshops) for the Paddington area in 1940. She 'soon found that the bombing was beginning to reduce the number of places on the books' (Tabb and Malins Smith p90). A 'dairy' turned out to have been taken over for grinding magnesium. Two chemical inspectors visited the premises within hours of receiving her report, putting the occupier 'into such a state of panic that action was taken long before regulations were made'. When 'the inevitable explosion' occurred, the firm wrote a letter of thanks, for the damage was slight and no-one had been hurt.

Prosecutions taken during these years usually followed accidents involving machinery. Miss Moorcroft points out:

🙶 One of the hazards of war time was the employment of 'green labour' in particular women who were unused to machinery and went into the factories for the first time. They were moreover working long hours which made them accident prone from sheer fatigue. 🙷 (Tabb and Malins Smith, p92)

New processes

A few years into the war, the duties of inspectors were further complicated, as Miss Moorcroft has recalled:

🙶 By 1941 the war was well and truly under way and new processes were taxing us to the full. The production of rubber dinghies and the lamination processes in the construction of aircraft gave rise to the use of new toxic solvents; factories were grossly overcrowded and mushroomed over night; the use of any space below ground which offered protection for personnel and plant, meant that work was being done in areas that were impossible to ventilate and often enough to heat. 🙷 (Tabb and Malins Smith, p91)

Marianne Woolgar recalls that the introduction of women factory workers in large numbers where women had not previously been employed meant inspectors had to pay special attention to sanitary facilities. One complaint she recalls was received from women workers in a cotton factory in Lancashire.

🙶 I think the Ministry of Supply realised that they hadn't got tropical suits and outfits for the servicemen and they had to start manufacturing them. The women were drafted back from the new modern Royal Ordnance Factories to this cotton textile factory to do this khaki drill, and there was a complaint, because the lavatories went off the main works (without a screen). Behind each door was embossed a notice 'Will ladies please adjust the back of their skirts before leaving'. It could have done with better lighting, better ventilation, but they must have spent an awful lot having these plaques made. 🙷 (interview with Marianne Wolgar, 1992)

Changed conditions for women inspectors

The special conditions of wartime also gave women inspectors the chance to do a wider range of inspecting work than had been usual before the war. Miss Vera Chinn recalls investigating an accident following the death of a woman crane driver, her first inspection involving mounting a crane. Miss Curry also recalled inspection work with cranes:

66 I had to get permission to wear trousers once. It was when women were ... starting driving overhead cranes, and I had to climb up. Elizabeth Parker (my senior) ... said, 'You can't possibly go during the day, there will be far too much confusion if they see you crawling about'. She said, 'Go on Sunday'. And I said, 'Well, look, can I wear my trousers?' So she said yes. So I went climbing up. 99 (interview with Norah Curry, 1992)

Women inspectors were not used completely interchangeably with men, however, even during the war, for Miss Curry remembers being moved from her Norwich posting 'because there was an immense building programme building airfields in Norfolk, and they thought they must have a man to cope with that, which was reasonable'. Anne Bettenson was also inspecting in a part of the country where similar work was going on. She has observed:

66 For most of the war years I was D I at either Lincoln or Cambridge and in the midst of the great expansion of the forward airfields - bomber stations, fighter stations, dispersal sites (to counter German attacks on the main fields) and then American bomber bases. In the later stages before D-Day some specialised inspectors were appointed to cover the particular problems of these sites, but the district staff were inevitably also involved.

The sites were largely constructed by Irish labour, mostly recruited from the Republic and housed in hutted camps far from any urban centre. Inspectors were charged with ensuring reasonable standards not only at work but also in the camps. There were no statutory requirements but various instructions on minimum standards were issued and we were expected to see that they were maintained. There was a good deal of sardonic mirth when a pompous circular required us to secure necessary conditions 'by sheer force of personality': frequent visits and general nagging were more likely means. 99 (Tabb and Malins Smith, p86-7)

Rationing and clothing coupons also brought special problems to women inspectors during the war. Norah Curry tells of how when Miss Messiter went on her summer holiday in 1941, her replacement Miss Barr arrived:

66 To my amazement she went inspecting without wearing stockings! I said to her 'Why do you not wear stockings?' And she said, 'Because of coupons!' I thought this was good, so I also started inspecting without wearing stockings. When Miss Messiter came back and saw my unstockinged legs, she said 'Stockings, please!' So I protested, and this matter was referred to the Superintending Inspector. But as the SI had allowed one of her staff to not wear stockings - one of her more senior staff - she said that I might be allowed to inspect without stockings. This was an important matter in the days when you had clothing coupons. 99 (interview with Norah Curry, 1992)

Miss Messiter had her own way of dealing with the risk of impropriety when climbing ladders in the course of inspecting. Dressed normally in 'a grey flannel suit, rather masculine design, and under it a white blouse with a black ribbon round it, the skirt very long', she would apparently safety pin the back to the front hem of her skirt when climbing a ladder. She 'wore a sort of pork pie hat', but not in the office. Miss Curry's reprimands from Miss Messiter with respect to dress did not end with the matter of stockings:

66 We'd been out inspecting one day together, and coming back in the train she said, 'Miss Curry, when you were climbing the ladder, I saw some bare flesh ABOVE the knee! I STRONGLY recommend knickers with elastic that cover the leg as far as the knee.' But I wasn't quite so subordinate that I took that advice! 99 (interview with Norah Curry 1992)

Because of the wartime conditions, a certain latitude in propriety seems to have been allowed during this period. Miss Curry recalls with some amazement that women inspectors, most of whom were single, both worked alongside and did firewatching duties with men inspectors most of whom were married:

66 I don't know how we got away with it! Nobody ever seemed to think it was peculiar. But on the whole, we never went inspecting at night with them. 99

The formidable Miss Alice Ewart, for whom Miss Curry worked during part of the war, appears to have taken a special interest in the welfare of her women junior inspectors. Norah Curry recalls that she assisted her in finding suitable accommodation and that after she was settled in a rented house with one of the canteen advisers, Margaret Bligh:

66 she used to come and visit us from time to time to see how we were getting on. ... Miss Ewart certainly had ideas that she should look after the women. 99

Accommodation problems seem to have been particularly acute for the women inspectors during the war. Their frequent moves, and the shortage of accommodation in circumstances when evacuation, billeting and bomb damage prevailed all combined to make this aspect of their lives trying. In addition, petrol rationing meant that bicycles had to be used, or public transport, wherever possible. Miss Moorcroft, out inspecting alone at night on foot, recalled:

66 I took the train to Queen's Park station in Kilburn and set off with the intention of working until the first train came into service in the small hours of the morning. Kilburn was not exactly salubrious and there was, of course, no street lighting in the blackout. I soon found I was being followed, not by anyone of evil intent, but by a kindly policeman who wanted to know what I was doing. I duly explained and he followed me for several hours, until he began to get rather tired of it. 'Look, Miss,' he said 'I know you are one of His Majesty's Inspectors of Factories, but I do wish you'd go' ome.' 99 (Tabb and Malins Smith, p94)

Miss Tabb took to using her bicycle to avoid the unpleasant conditions of travel on tube trains during the war. Her bicycle also seemed the best way of getting about while attempting to fulfil one of the Factory Department's more unreasonable requests during the war:

66 We were asked by HQ to estimate the number of square feet of glass which had been broken in factories, but after a preliminary survey (at ½d a mile)

I decided it was easier to sit in the office and think of a number. " " (Tabb and Malins Smith p94)

In the latter part of the war, Marianne Woolgar was in London, having asked to be moved nearer to where her children were living. This gave her the opportunity to witness the scenes in London as the end of this difficult and dangerous period was celebrated, and she recalls that on VE Day she 'wandered around London', 'saw Churchill at close quarters', watched the 'returning boys' coming back from concentration camps in Germany, and 'was in the cheering crowds outside Buckingham Palace when the Royal Family came out on the balcony'. It must have been an emotional day for her: like other women inspectors, she had seen much of the privation and suffering which the war had brought to the population working at home; and the contribution which she had made had been given while she adjusted to her altered circumstances as a war widow. For her, the post war years were to bring a special distinction: in 1957 she became the first woman Chemical Inspector of Factories.

Chapter Five

Women Factory Inspectors in an era of rapid technological change

The years following the end of the Second World War in 1945 were not easy ones for the Factory Department, and women factory inspectors, like their male counterparts, did not experience a rapid amelioration of their working situation. Post-war reconstruction, shortages of materials and of workers, including continuing staffing problems in the Inspectorate, combined to make these years almost as demanding of inspectors as the war years had been.

Miss F I Taylor

Miss F I Taylor

The senior woman in the Inspectorate was still, in 1945, Miss F Isabel (Fanny) Taylor. She had succeeded Miss Martindale in 1933 and had played an important role in the work of the Inspectorate as one of the Deputy Chief Inspectors. Her contributions to the annual reports included regular chapters about the enforcement of hours of employment regulations, a topic on which she was an expert, having been a member of several Home Office Committees on matters associated with hours of employment in the 1930s. Miss Taylor is vividly remembered by those women inspectors who worked with her. Unlike some of her predecessors, she did not leave her own detailed memoirs, for she died unexpectedly and after only a very short illness in 1947, while still in post.

After her death, the Chief Inspector included the following tribute to MissTaylor in his Annual Report for 1947:

66 The Department was shocked by the sudden passing of Miss F I Taylor, CBE, the senior Deputy Chief Inspector, after a very short illness. Miss Taylor had been at Headquarters since 1933 and was an authority of international repute on questions concerning the employment of women and young persons and the development of welfare in industry. The loss of her wise counsel, shrewd judgement and wide knowledge of so many of the problems of industry came as a severe blow to the Department ... Through her work in the conduct of various negotiations under the aegis of the International Labour Office during conferences at Geneva and Montreal, she was personally known to many in other countries and her presence at international meetings will be sadly missed. 99 (ARCI, 1947 p105)

Cecily Tabb worked with Miss Taylor in the immediate postwar years during her own posting to Central Office. She recalls her as efficient and considerate, though a little intimidating to a young inspector:

66 I worked with her on Emergency Orders which were still being issued. She was very easy to work for, in that she said, 'You have all the papers. Come and ask me if you can't deal with them.' She was very calm and well balanced, and a VERY quick thinker. I remember taking one lot of papers to her, and giving her the gist of what I wanted to know: she told me at once what to do. I said, 'But you haven't read the papers yet!' And she said, 'I've made the decision, and that's what matters.' She didn't dither at all. Once when she said 'I'm going for a minor operation this afternoon', I said 'Oh, I am sorry' - I didn't know she meant a hairdo! It made me realise that Fanny was really human. 99 (interview with Cecily Tabb 1992)

Miss D Johnson

Other senior women in the years just after the war included Miss D Johnson, who would succeed Miss Taylor, and who had been responsible for organising the work of the Canteen Advisory Service. The canteen advisers' work had been well received during the war, and the service was retained until 1956: Miss Johnson's efficiency in this role had been widely recognised, although she seems also to have been rather formidable. Norah Curry recalls hearing about 'how she ruled her poor canteen advisers with a rod of iron' (interview with Norah Curry 1992), and Cecily Tabb remembers her as someone with 'a lot of drive, a lot of brain' but a rather 'volatile' nature. Miss Johnson occupied the post of Deputy Chief Inspector until her retirement in December 1955, and like several of the women inspectors who had gone before her, was honoured with the award of the CBE.

Recruitment

In 1947 the Chief Inspector reported that inspectors in post had numbered 314, a full 100 below the authorised establishment of 414. Steps were taken during the year to rectify the situation, and 75 candidates were selected through the selection boards under the Reconstruction Competition. Twenty five of these began work in December 1947 (some were former temporary inspectors) and the remainder were due to start in 1948.

Indeed, throughout the post war years, up until about 1970, the Chief Inspector regularly reported difficulties in recruiting suitably qualified staff, and the Inspectorate was below strength for almost all of this period. In the immediate aftermath of the war, many of the inspectors who had been on the temporary staff during the war were available for permanent establishment. Those, like Marianne Woolgar, who were over 30 years old were allowed to become established without sitting the Civil Service examination, although as Dr Woolgar recalls, they were subjected to 'a very stiff boarding'. The younger temporary inspectors were, however, required to sit an examination alongside candidates who had no previous service in the Factory Department. Norah Curry recalled that there was some resentment about the way the younger temporary inspectors, of whom she was one, were treated. The Department was not permitted to make permanent recruitment to established posts until 1947; after successfully overcoming the examination hurdle, those who had worked during the war felt that they might be entitled to relatively swift promotion. In fact this does not seem to have been the case, and Norah Curry recalls:

66 In 1950 ... there were a group of women who had been temporary inspectors and we all thought we ought to have got our promotion to lB, and we agitated among each other. And then some did and some didn't, and we got even crosser. And then of course these new recruits, these new people, who were the same age as us but without our experience of inspection, were getting promoted before we were. So there was a certain amount of discontent about that. Some of the temporary inspectors were men, but most were women. And I think quite a lot of men were in the over 30 group that sailed through, and then of course got promotion immediately. So they did very well, but we got rather cross. 99 (interview with Norah Curry, 1992)

The difficulty which women seem to have experienced in gaining promotion during this period has some significance, for it helps to explain why it was in the 1950s, after so many years of successfully retaining a senior position for a woman inspector, that there should be a period when women appeared to lose their place.

Miss D Johnson

Women inspectors' work

At this time women were essentially doing the same work as men, although as Miss Tabb recalls there were still restrictions:

66 Of course, women weren't supposed to go to docks and shipyards or places where men worked with little or nothing on. We weren't supposed to go to building sites, or shipyards and docks. I suppose it was (because of) climbing ladders - we didn't wear trousers in those days. 99 (interview with Cecily Tabb, 1992)

Janet Wilson, who began inspecting in 1967, also commented on this aspect in her short account of women factory inspectors:

66 The Secretary of State's instructions to inspectors shortly after reorganisation specified three areas which should remain the special responsibility of men inspectors. These were heavy industries ..., places where men had to work in scanty clothing ..., and places where inspection involves the climbing of ladders to considerable height ... 99 (Wilson, 1983 p20)

Apart from this, however, women who were inspectors in the 1940s and 1950s recall very little difference in the work done by men and women. There were differences in pay (of which more later) and it was already clear that women were not coming into the specialist areas of inspection (see following chapter), but as Anne Bettenson, who inspected between 1930 and 1965, put it:

66 The Factory Inspectorate gave equality of work to women long before many other branches of work which would on the face of it seem more suitable and I think it should be put on record, how little trouble women inspectors of my generation suffered from overt prejudice in carrying out their duties 99 (Tabb and Malins Smith p49).

Cecily Tabb recalls that 'the men and women around me were on good terms', and that when she took her first prosecution, her woman DI (Miss D Dunch) did not think to accompany her, but one of her male colleagues asked 'Would you like me to come?' to which she replied, 'Well, yes, frankly I would.'

Loss of the senior woman's post

When Miss Johnson, Deputy Chief Inspector, retired on December 20th 1955 no woman was appointed to replace her. The field from which a female candidate could have been drawn was limited, and essentially comprised four women then in the post of Superintending Inspector:

Miss E Schofield (born 3.9.1892)

Miss K Crundwell (born 1.10.1898)
Miss V E Chinn (born 6.10.1898)
Miss A S Bettenson (born 1905)

The first three of these were possibly considered suitably qualified but too old to be appointed to a DCI post (a point made by Miss Curry). Miss Bettenson had only recently been promoted to SI (in September 1955) and was unlikely to be thought sufficiently experienced for such an appointment. The decision to appoint a man to the vacant post was therefore understandable, and defensible in certain terms. But it was also deeply resented by some of the women inspectors. A document protesting against the decision, and urging that the situation be rectified when the next DCI post fell vacant (on the expected retirement of one of the DCIs the following year) was prepared. It argued:

❝ Conditions to-day are very similar to what they were in 1928. The duties of the men and women inspectors continue to be common to men and women. The proportion of men to women has only increased to 22% and has not reached the 30% which ... was recommended by the 1928 Committee. There are 282 men and 80 women inspectors to-day. There are about 10 million men and 5 million women in industry today.

The reasons the 1928 Committee gave for reserving a DCI post for a woman are equally applicable today.

No reason, however, has been given for the departure from this long established practice of having a woman Deputy Chief Inspector of Factories at Headquarters. Any contention that the reservation of this post for a woman is no longer necessary because of the establishment of equal pay or a common seniority list cannot be accepted because:

1)   Equal pay has not been established and will not be established for another 6 years.

2)   There can be no common seniority list where the proportion of women to men is so small.

3)   There has not been a completely fair field or equal opportunity as in the past senior women have not been eligible for all senior posts as they became vacant. For many, many years only two SI posts, then three, and only recently four, have been available to women. ❞

The document goes on to point out that three of the Superintending Inspector posts reserved for women (three out of 12) were in specified areas - Southern Division (where Miss Schofield was the SI in 1955); East Midlands Division (where Miss Chinn was SI in 1955), and West Midlands Division (where Miss Crundwell was SI in 1955). Only at the end of the Second World War had a fourth post, in the North Western Division, been given to a woman, and it was to this post that Miss Bettenson had recently been appointed. With the creation of a 13th Division (Wales) at the end of the war, women now occupied only four out of 13 SI posts. This situation, with only four women but nine men eligible candidates for promotion, was seen as not offering equality of opportunity, and justifying the case for continuing to reserve a DCI post for a woman.

The argument was put, and a question was asked in the House of Commons, but not accepted. Miss Johnson's retirement was followed by the appointment of an engineer, Mr R Bramley Harker, and the vacancy which arose on the retirement of a man in April 1956 was filled in May of that year by Mr J MacColl. It was not until April 1959 that another woman, Miss K Crundwell, was appointed DCI. Her appointment then, at the age of 60, somewhat invalidates the suggestion that at the earlier point, to which the complaint relates, she was too old to be appointed.

Miss A Bettenson

Unequal pay

Miss Chinn, who retired in 1960, commented in her interview that 'she never had equal pay'. The detailed evidence on rates of pay up until then certainly bears her out, and so the way the issue of men's and women's pay developed after 1945 deserves some attention. The official staff list of the Factory Department issued in 1954 gives information about rates of pay in the grades where both men and women were employed (see below).

There were, then, marked pay differentials between men and women at almost all levels: at DCI, SI and Inspector Class 1A and 1B, although the most junior factory inspector grades had equal pay. There was sex discrimination in pay rates for canteen advisers, too, but not for medical inspectors. One of the two Deputy Senior Medical Inspectors, and two of the eleven medical inspectors, were women. The rates of pay for medical inspectors were set high (presumably in parity with the medical profession) in any case. In 1954 no women were employed as specialist inspectors.

Equal pay had been on the agenda of women factory inspectors for some years. Hilda Martindale

Chief Inspector:	£2,225
Deputy Chief Inspector:	£2,000 (men)
	£1,825(women)
Superintending Inspector:	£1,375 x£50 - £1,475 x £75 - £1,675 (men)
	£1,200 x £50 - £1,500 (women)
	plus Pay Addition, men and women
Senior Medical Inspector:	£2,300
Deputy Senior Medical Inspector:	£2,200 (men and women)
Medical Inspector:	£1,500 (age 35) x £75 - £1,800 x £100 - £2,100 (men and women)
Inspector, Class 1A:	£910 x £30 - £1,000 x £40 - £1,200 x £50 - £1,325 (men)
	£800 x £30 - £980 x £40 - £1,150 (women)
	plus Pay Addition, men and women
Inspector, Class lB:	£740 x £30 - £1,025 (men)
	£740 x £30 - £925 (women) plus Pay Addition
Inspector, Class 11 and Temporary Inspector:	£365 (at 21) x £25 - £490 (at 26) x £25 - £685 (men and women) plus Pay Addition.
Senior Canteen Adviser:	£875 x £30 - £995 x £40 - £1,050 plus Pay Addition (women)
Canteen Advisers:	£740 x £30 - 915 (men)
	£615 x £25 - £740 x £30 - £795 (women)
	Plus Pay Addition (men and women)

Dr Marianne Woolgar

had been interested in the issue during her time as DCI, and while at the Treasury in the mid 1930s had been able to press for equal pay on several important committees. Professional women and civil servants generally had been agitating about this issue before the war, but in the postwar period the government held the view that although equal pay was desirable, the economy could not afford it.

A campaign for equal pay in the civil service had been begun in earnest in 1951: that year the Staff Side of the Civil Service National Whitley Council committed itself to fight for equal pay, and the Institution of Professional Civil Servants also pledged its support (Boston, 1980 p249). The campaign culminated in a petition, signed by 600,000 people, presented at the House of Commons in March 1954; within a fortnight the Chancellor of the Exchequer was promising that equal pay 'was on its way' (Boston, 1980 p250). Early in 1955 the timetable for implementation was announced:

❝ The agreed timetable was to reduce the gap in seven stages by means of seven annual increments - the first backdated to January 1955 - to give women equal pay on 1 January 1961. ❞ (Boston, 1980 p250-1)

Marianne Woolgar remembers the campaign. She had attended meetings of the Council of Women Civil Servants during the war, and had met Hilda Martindale there. In celebration of the introduction of graduated equal pay, she now attended the Milestone Dinner, held (she thinks) at the Savoy Hotel. Special guests "included Lord and Lady Pakenham, Jennie Lee, Philippa Strachey (the last surviving suffragette) and David Eccles, the then Minister of Education".

Although they were aware of inequalities in pay during these years, retired inspectors suggest that there was not widespread resentment about the issue among women in the Inspectorate. Miss Tabb pointed out that she felt "thankful to have any money at all"; while Norah Curry recalls feeling when she started work as an inspector that:

❝ for somebody my age it was marvellous. I thought I was rolling. You started with £275. I felt I was doing well compared to all my friends and relations. ❞ (interview with Norah Curry, 1992)

Women's place in the Inspectorate

The 1954 staff list indicates that in that year there were 80 women inspectors plus 18 women in the canteen advisory grades and two women in the medical inspector grades. Of these, seven women factory inspectors (none above the grade of Inspector Class 1A), three canteen advisers and one medical inspector were married women or widows at that time.

A record of staff in post in 1973 shows for the Divisions (excluding Scotland) and the London Headquarters 46 women inspectors. Audrey Pittom was in the post of Deputy Chief Inspector, but there were no women Superintending Inspectors in England and Wales, and only two women Deputy Superintending Inspectors (Miss Tabb and Miss Moorcroft). Women occupied 10 of the 102 posts of District Inspector (excluding Scotland). The proportion of those in the inspectorial grades who were women had declined markedly since 1954, with the 30% share anticipated in 1930 never achieved.

Domestic circumstances

Women working as inspectors during this period were, as in the years before 1939, mostly single, childless women. Dr Woolgar, as a widow with two children, was exceptional, and as late as 1935 and 1937 the Chief Inspector's Annual Report indicates that women were retiring from the Factory Department on marriage: Miss R C Viret and Miss B M Davies both retired as Class II inspectors on these grounds in 1935 and 1937 respectively. By 1973 (before the term 'Ms' came into general usage) 10 of the 46 women inspectors are listed as 'Mrs'.

Women factory inspectors, then, were throughout this period mostly single women. It would, however, be inaccurate to depict them as 'without domestic responsibilities', for although most did not have a husband and family, a number did have quite onerous responsibilities towards elderly or infirm parents, and in some cases this situation probably limited their career prospects. Miss Curry, who lived with her widowed mother from 1950 until 1965, recalls that after her father died in 1949, she negotiated about her domestic situation with the department:

66 I said, 'Look, I've got to make a home for my mother somewhere, and I'd like to move somewhere where I can be for a good long time'. So he said, 'If I move you to Bradford, and you get somewhere where you can get to Bradford or to Leeds I can pretty well promise you when you've finished your spell in Bradford you can go to Leeds.' So I set up house with my mother. ... She was OK while we were in Yorkshire, but in the modern day I don't think they'd have moved me (to London) in 1962, when she was 79. I think I'd complain. 99

Other women inspectors had more difficult domestic problems. Katharine Malins Smith was one promising inspector who 'in the middle of her career' got held up because of domestic problems, and Miss Betty Horsfall at one time 'came down most weekends from Aberdeen to Ilkley to care for her parents. (interview with Norah Curry 1992)

The remarkable Miss Bessie Blackburn lived

with her father for many years after he was widowed. They first 'set up housekeeping together' in 1934, shortly after her mother's death, and lived together until 1959 when Mr William Blackburn died:

66 We decided that from my salary I would pay William a housekeeping allowance and he would take over the house and cooking of the meals, Monday to Friday. This was his suggestion as he knew factory inspection could be very hard going and he did not want me to be overworked. He soon learned to cook and became a better cook than me. 99 (Blackburn, no date p36)

The personalities of women who inspected during the postwar decades suggest that women factory inspectors in these years shared certain characteristics, but also differed quite considerably from one another. Norah Curry emphasises that 'there was as much range in the women, between their techniques, as there was with the men' (interview with Norah Curry 1992). A few sketches of some of the more outstanding personalities may indicate that these women were every bit as remarkable as their predecessors the Lady Inspectors.

Miss F E Messiter

Miss Messiter, who rose to the rank of Deputy Superintending Inspector, has already been mentioned. Her 'questing spirit and zestful work for accident prevention' were noted in the preface to the re-printed edition of her *Study of the Operations at Unfenced Machinery Regulations* (1959). Norah Curry worked under Miss Messiter on several occasions, and holds her responsible for her failure to meet the legendary Miss Martindale:

66 Miss Martindale was coming down to see Miss Messiter, and we all thought 'Oh, golly, we're going to see this famous lady!' But Miss Messiter was so determined to show Miss Martindale what a good

office she ran, she told us all we had to be out inspecting, and not come near the office. It was a great pity because it would have been nice to have seen her. I'd have loved to have met her. 99 (interview with Norah Curry 1992)

When she was working in Ilford just after the war, with Miss Messiter as her superior, Miss Curry recalls having her work very carefully checked and scrutinised. As a junior:

66 You spent a day a week writing your reports, and you spent a long time going through your report with Miss Messiter. 99

Miss K M Haddock

In January 1962 Miss Curry took up a posting at Headquarters which brought her into contact with another remarkable woman. Miss Haddock (born 1911) became legendary within the Inspectorate

for her contribution to the more efficient administration of the Department. Miss Curry explains:

66 And then I was working for Miss Haddock. I must tell you about her - (she) did an amazing job.

Now it looks absolutely primaeval ... but at the time she moved the Inspectorate into a better system for reporting visits and recording information and issuing instructions. **Before** her day ... the Chief Inspector sent out a monthly circular, and it was all in paragraphs on different topics. ... And some poor clerical officer had one of these copies and cut it up and filed them under the appropriate heading. 〞

Miss Haddock changed all this, so that subsequently 'we had individual instructions on individual sheets sent out'. She also altered 'the enormous registers (which) got in a terrible mess ... to something more flexible', and also arranged for there to be:

〝 files for firms, which we could take out when we went to inspect them. And in these files were placed copies of all the letters we'd sent. ... It was **primitive** before. She had implemented all this with (Miss Boyde), who died, and so then I was sent up there. I think they probably didn't have available on the list a man who they would regard as as literate as I was. After all, I had a Girton degree as an historian, so I ought to be able to put some instructions together. They wouldn't be wasting the powers of a man who was an engineer or a chemist or something like that. 〞 (interview with Norah Curry 1992)

She was 'a demon for work', and Norah Curry

remembers 'I often wouldn't get away until about 7' because of the long hours Miss Haddock worked. However, she was kind and helpful when Miss Curry's mother died, and gave her good support if there were problems with the work. Miss Curry explained:

〝 All instructions went out through me. I was responsible for seeing that they were coherent and logical and capable of being carried out. A lot of them when they first arrived on my desk were far from that! ... If I had any problems, she'd see the Chief Inspector, and say, 'Look, we can't send out these incoherent stammerings - they must think out what they want.' 〞 (interview with Norah Curry 1992)

In the late 1960s, Miss Haddock had been promoted to Deputy Superintending Inspector at Divisional Headquarters and was in her late 50s. Among her responsibilities was the training of new inspectors. Janet Wilson, who was recruited in 1967, recalls:

〝 She always wore a shirt and tie - this was **not** typical of women inspectors - and drove a sports car. I always made sure my office window was open when she came as she was a fresh air fiend and thought she had a convert in me. I was told to wear a hat for inspection: I wore a black woolly thing for about two weeks and then stopped. 〞

Sadly, Miss Haddock was killed in a car accident soon after she retired.

Dress

The conventions about dress to which women inspectors adhered were beginning to change at around the time Janet Wilson was recruited. The taboo on wearing trousers lasted until the 1970s, but hats were becoming dispensable by about that time. The picture of Miss Massey inspecting in Nottingham (overleaf) shows clearly her rather plain suit and hat. Miss Chinn, who was Marion

Miss Massey tracks down workshop perils

by DON EVERITT

It may be bad lighting—or it may be poisonous gas. One factory looked like something out of Dickens. And that's when Marion Massey may pay a surprise visit

TALL, FAIR AND DEMURE, Marion Massey is a Lancastrian whose job requires her to investigate startling and often gory deaths and injuries. Once, she was called to a factory where two men had been killed in the boilerhouse. Reconstructing the events leading to the tragedy, she found that the boilerman had opened the blow-down valve to eject sediment into the pit beneath the boiler. When he came to close the valve, it would not move. Desperately, stubbornly, he struggled with it as scalding steam hissed into the boilerhouse. The boilerman's mate dashed in, but it was too late; the boilerman collapsed, and before his mate could drag him to safety the steam overcame him, too.

To examine the blow-down, Marion Massey donned overalls, got underneath the boiler and dismantled the valve. Inside she found a one-inch nut, tightly wedged. "It had been left in the boiler after a recent scaling," she explains. "When the boilerman opened the valve, the nut dropped in and jammed it."

Such industrial detective work is part of Marion Massey's everyday routine as one of Her Majesty's inspectors of factories. In the latest recorded year, Britain's 350-strong inspectorate reported on more than 800 fatalities and 180,000 injuries.

Garage Gas Jet Exploded

"In investigating accidents," Marion Massey says, "we have to find out the causes and whether anyone has contravened the Factories Acts; more important, we have to suggest measures to prevent recurrences." Ironically, the preventive steps taken after many industrial accidents are so simple that at times they appear superfluous: this is because a good proportion of the accidents result from human, not mechanical, frailty.

Some time ago, a garage hand was repairing a petrol tank taken from a car. To clean out all the petrol, he held the intake under a tap and ran hot water through the outlet. Suddenly, a violent explosion shook the garage and badly injured the man. Marion Massey says: "The explanation was obvious as soon as we went through the door. Above the tap was a gas geyser. The water had forced petrol vapour out of the tank and an inflammable mixture had risen into the gas jet.'

On another occasion, a young man died at a laboratory sink while cleaning his hands with cyanide after silvering glass. When the sink trap was unscrewed, traces of acid were found. "Someone had poured acid down the sink before the man had used the cyanide. Some of the acid had stayed in the trap, mixed with the cyanide, and a few whiffs of the resulting gas had poisoned the man within seconds."

What Marion Massey did afterwards was to

A seat should be just the right height. So should the footrest. In this Boots' factory at Nottingham, Miss Massey checks for comfort. Inspectors find most managements willing to co-operate

29

Massey's Superintending Inspector at the time when this photograph was taken, recalled 'You wore a suit and hat - oh yes, and good shoes. We all wore hats then.' (interview with Vera Chinn 1992)

Miss E J Forrest (born 1894) was Norah Curry's District Inspector in Bradford just after the war. She 'always wore a hat - in the office. She was a very dignified sort of lady who sort of sailed round factories'. Others whose appearance attracted comment included Miss McWilliam, who was 'IMMACULATELY turned out always - every hair in place...she was one of the toughest'. (interview with Norah Curry 1992)

Technological changes

Inspection in the postwar decades involved getting to grips with very rapid change, especially after the initial period of shortages and reconstruction was over. The work of inspection became ever more complex, and with this came the development in inspection of specialist branches: these are described in more detail in the following chapter. The Chief Inspector's Annual Reports indicate the stages at which particular developments became important for inspectors. In 1952 there is special mention of industrial developments in electricity supply and the use of electricity. Progressively the proportion of factories without power was becoming smaller. There is also mention that year of radiological applications to industrial processes, and automation in factories is mentioned for the first time in the 1954 Annual Report.

In 1955 comment is passed on the design of factory buildings, and there is reference to the 'erection of modern flatted buildings in which to rehouse small firms occupying old and unsuitable premises' in congested urban districts. Inspectors played their role in giving advice about safety problems and how difficulties could be foreseen and eradicated at the design stage. Unfortunately it is difficult, because of the anonymous way in which these Annual Reports are framed, to know precisely what part women played in monitoring these developments.

The work of factory inspectors during this period comprised essentially the same elements which had been important before the war, but carried out in a more complex technological working environment. Inspectors were there to enforce factory legislation, using advice, persuasion, monitoring and when necessary prosecution as their chief weapons against unsafe working conditions. There was some important new legislation during this time; some of the traditional concerns of earlier generations of inspectors, such as enforcement of the Truck Acts, gradually faded away; while fire prevention, guarding of machinery, safe use of toxic substances old and new and the supervision of working hours remained firmly on the agenda. There were new developments in industrial welfare, some springing from wartime experience, and there were continuing and developing contacts with factory inspectors and others concerned with workplace safety in other countries and as part of international obligations.

This book cannot provide a systematic review of all of these developments. However, they have been touched on by those women inspectors who have put their own memories and experiences on record. Their work was not, except in the ways already mentioned, very different from that of men inspectors, and some of those who have contributed to this book wanted to emphasise that a focus on women inspectors in the centenary year should not be taken as a claim that women were better inspectors than men.

Legislation and enforcement

During the postwar period, up until the major changes introduced by the Health and Safety at Work etc Act 1974, there were several important new pieces of legislation, and numerous minor amendments to the law, some introduced through Orders and Regulations. The 1948 Factory Act, the Factories Acts of 1959 and 1961 and the 1963 Offices, Shops and Railway Premises Act, all brought important changes, the latter considerably widening the field of inspection.

While more legislation clearly meant more and more complicated work for factory inspectors, some areas of work were being redesignated as outside the scope of the Factory Department. The promotion of personnel management in industry had developed during the war, culminating in 1946 with the appointment of Miss D McWilliam to take charge of the Personnel Management Branch, with its staff of nine. However in 1940 the Branch was transferred out of the Factory Department to the Industrial Relations Department of the Ministry of Labour, the Ministry in which the Factory Department had been decisively placed after the war under legislation passed in 1946.

What women inspectors recall about the legislation of this period is of course the more interesting and dramatic incidents which arose in its enforcement. Miss Curry recalled vividly her first prosecution, which followed the investigation of an accident during her time in Ilford. She had kept a press clipping from the local newspaper which both gave an account of the case, and mentioned her by name.

Other types of contravention which often led to prosecutions were the failure to guard and fence machinery securely, and the excessive employment of women and young persons.

Several inspectors felt that it was in court in particular that they had met sexual discrimination. Miss Curry commented:

❝ There was a stipendiary magistrate in Leeds who didn't like women inspectors. He always seemed to be much more acid. 'Are you here to prosecute?' And also later on when I was in Bethnal Green the stipendiary magistrate in the magistrates' court was extremely difficult. It even got to the point that one of the DCIs came down to hear me taking a case, to just make sure that I wasn't being unduly aggressive or something.

You always felt at a disadvantage with both of them because you were a woman. Neither of the courts seemed to have women court officials. I think most of the women of my era would say that they were made well aware that stipendiary magistrates at any rate didn't take to having women. Of course they didn't like factory inspectors anyway. ... We always took our own prosecutions because there were powers for that in the Factories Acts. That was a preliminary hurdle that all inspectors had to get over - that the courts weren't used to us. And then when you were a woman on top of it, it did make life slightly more difficult. ❞ (interview with Norah Curry 1992)

Accidents, such as the one which led to Miss Curry's first prosecution, were of course a continuing source of work for inspectors. In the Annual Report for 1947, the Chief Inspector noted:

❝ Many cases of women and girls having their hair entangled in machinery have been reported. Drill chucks, including those used for tapping, stock bars and machine spindles, have been largely responsible but shafting has caused several distressing accidents. Two of the shafting accidents related to women who, climbing on benches to open windows, allowed their hair to go in the vicinity of overhead shafts. The shafts gathered up their hair and completely scalped the women. ❞ (ARCI, 1947 p31)

It was in fact in 1947 that the statistics for accidents began to return to their prewar level. Figure 2 from the Annual Report for 1953 (p28) shows this change, and clearly depicts the marked increase in accidents to all types of industrial worker during the war years.

Dr Woolgar explained her feelings about some of the fatal accidents she was involved in investigating:

❝ You'd go to an inquest, and then (if) the firm were in breach of the Factories Act ... the case would come along afterwards and you'd take a prosecution. And the FINE in those days would be £25 for the life of a breadwinner! I used to be so angry about this.

The first inquest I ever took was a woman who died of aplastic anaemia after working with benzine solution for 18 months. It was rubber solution with benzine: the firm had complied with the regulations, so the work was done under mechanically exhausted cowl, but they didn't build a knee-box for her knees! ... Time and again you'd find these daft arrangements, where the person couldn't get near enough. Instead of doing the work under the enclosure, she sat out because she couldn't get her knees under, and she was inhaling the vapour. 99 (interview with Marianne Woolgar 1992)

Fires were another type of incident vividly recalled by the retired inspectors. The dramatic nature of fires, and the fact that loss of life could be severe, perhaps explains why these occurrences are so clearly remembered even many years later. Miss Curry worked as District Inspector in Bethnal

Green between 1966 and 1971. She recalls:

66 It was all small workshops - clothing, foam plastic upholstery. This was the time of all the concern about foam plastic - because there had been fires - and the Chief Inspector told me that there were more upholstery factories in Bethnal Green than in the whole of the south of England. So we spent a lot of time visiting these factories and trying to improve fire precautions. 99

Asked how successful she felt this work had been Miss Curry replied:

66 We probably killed them all off with asbestos instead! Because we were advising them to put up asbestos screens to protect their stairways and things like that. Actually I think that what we were doing was good, and wasn't dangerous, except if people were handling it badly - sawing it up without protection. We prosecuted several firms for contravention of fire regulations. 99 (interview with Norah Curry 1992)

Dangerous substances

Another substance which was coming into widespread use during these years, and causing an increased fire hazard, was celluloid. This substance had been identified as a serious fire risk in the 1930s, when Miss Hastings had reported on the highly dangerous conditions in which young girls cutting up used cinematograph film were working. (ARCI, 1930 p38)

Now, in the postwar period, similar conditions were found again. Dr Woolgar:

66 In 1947 when I was in the Richmond District there was a disastrous fire and an inquiry. It was a scrap merchants' place - in the early days for the cinematograph film, before the safety-based film, the cellulose acetate, was in full use. This was a kind of warehouse where the women during the day sorted the acetate from the nitrate, and this dreadful fire started at night. It was a very hot summer and ... the cellulose nitrate punchings from the roll film - there were

quite a lot of those, because they were used for making cellulose solution - had fallen between the wooden floorboard cracks (and self ignited). They had four storage units that were built to meet the requirements of the cinematograph regulations for storing the reels of film, but the fire was so hot the heat was transmitted through iron doors ... and the reels of film inside of course exploded. They were blown up out of the factory, and on the other side of the road was another factory where they were using cellulose solutions, and that set alight. There was a house adjoining, and four children were burnt to death there - the mother and four children, and also a woman in another house who ran out on the road that was ablaze. And **I** was the last inspector to have visited this place!

I was inspecting in Guildford, and I got a paper, and I saw this - 'Fire in Richmond'. It was a terrible feeling to think - 'Good heavens, did I miss something?' 🙶

One of the critical factors in this incident had been a faulty sprinkler system. The inquiry revealed that during the previous hard winter 'the main valve of their sprinkler system froze and cracked' - a new one had been ordered but had not yet arrived. The inquiry agreed that in the circumstances the factory inspector had not been negligent. Nevertheless this incident made Dr Woolgar ever more vigilant about celluloid:

🙶 In those days the sides of vehicles were celluloid - and the canvas roofs that the little Austins had - and motorcycle screens. So in all the garages, motor vehicle repair premises - you always asked them what they did and where they stored their celluloid! 🙶 (interview with Marianne Woolgar 1992)

All of the dangers associated with asbestos, which Miss Curry and other inspectors were urging occupiers to install as a protection against fire, were not at this time recognised and understood. Risks associated with its use had begun to be noticed at the start of the century by inspectors, and Lady Inspectors had made important observations about it. Miss Tabb now had contact with this substance in her inspection work:

🙶 There wasn't much asbestos used in any of my districts. At one factory that made plasterboard containing asbestos, the manager tried to reassure me about the clouds coming from the presses, saying 'Oh, all that cloud, that's just steam'. He may have been right but I had no means of checking. It wasn't till I got to Birmingham (in 1964) that there was asbestos in the Lucas factory in the accumulator cases. It was a problem. Not so much our problem, as the legislation. Because once they make Regulations, it takes over from the main requirement of the Act. I didn't know how awful (asbestos) was. I never saw a case of asbestosis - a man with splayed fingers - I did see quite a lot of widows of men who died of silicosis or pneumoconiosis - who'd worked in foundries and fettled castings which carried some risk. 🙶 (interview with Norah Curry 1992)

In May 1969 new Asbestos Regulations were made (ARCI, 1969 p35). These replaced the Asbestos Industry Regulations of 1931, and introduced more stringent conditions for protecting workers against asbestos dust.

Miss Alice Crossthwaite was among the first factory inspectors in this period to identify the very serious further hazards which asbestos is now known to pose, especially the risk of the disease mesothelioma which can develop after contact with blue asbestos dust. After making observations in a factory in her district she wanted to bring a prosecution, but was not allowed to do so. Later that factory was the subject of a prosecution, which drew attention to this new risk, and led to the extensive precautions which are nowadays taken. (interview with Norah Curry 1992)

Hours of employment

Hours of employment regulations still occupied an important place in the duties of factory inspectors during these years. The restrictions on the hours which all workers, but especially women and young persons, could legally work, affected the length of the working day and working week: night and Sunday work for women was still banned except where special exemptions had been granted. The Chief Inspector's Annual Reports show that hours of work remained an important source of complaints and prosecutions, such as one which Miss Curry took against a Baildon firm in the early 1950s.

There were also important changes in the hours of women's employment during this period, especially the development of part-time work among married women and the introduction of the double shift system. There was now a gradual development among inspectors of a view that protective or restrictive legislation limiting women's hours of employment was not necessarily a good thing. In 1949 the Chief Inspector indicated that the 1937 Factory Act was perhaps too inflexible on this question:

66 Where women were found illegally employed it was nearly always with their full agreement. Indeed the impatience of many women workers with restraints on their employment has been manifested more strongly than ever. With the security of full employment they feel impatient with protective legislation which sometimes prevents them from rendering in their opinion the most advantageous use of their own skill and the arrangement of hours most convenient to their own domestic affairs. ... They would often prefer to put in a few hours overtime on Sunday rather than on Saturday morning and in many Districts, particularly in the North and in Scotland, they prefer to work off all their overtime allowance under the 1937 Factory Act in two days in the week and leave the other evenings free for personal affairs. 99 (ARCI, 1949 p166)

Nevertheless some serious illegal employment was also found, examples of children under school-leaving age working in laundries and small factories in agricultural areas being particularly noted.

Welfare

Other concerns about the welfare of workers are revealed in what now seem rather amusing comments in the Annual Report:

" More interest in clothing accommodation is shown by women than by men. Objection was raised to a new cloakroom separated from a messroom by a 7 ft high partition; the women said their coats would smell of fish and chips. Having their belongings in handbags in the workrooms, instead of in coat pockets, makes women less anxious about possible pilfering. More firms are now providing suitable accommodation within workrooms for handbags, so that they will not be laid on machines, on workbenches or on the floor and possibly cause accidents. "

Managements employing married women realise that the arrival at work of shopping bags and baskets is inevitable, and are accordingly arranging that these, too, be suitably housed. (ARCI, 1955 p238)

International activities

Inspectors in the postwar period continued to play their part in international affairs relating to industrial health and safety. In 1947, Miss Vera Chinn was chosen to represent the Factory Department and was one of a very small number of women in the British delegation making a return visit to Paris. She recalls:

" We went on the Blue Arrow, first class - they had the silver service out and all that - and we stayed about a quarter of a mile from the British Embassy. We got invited there to a do - it was Lady Diana Manners and her husband. Then we were taken to a couple of big car manufacturers. When it was May Day ... they decided to take us up the coast and show us some of the war landing places. And we got to Rouen ... and we started lunch at 12 o'clock and we finished at 5 o'clock! (Later) we went back to Paris and went on to see some of these other factories. I enjoyed that very much. " (interview with Vera Chinn 1992)

Miss Taylor, who died while Miss Chinn was in Paris, was also prominent on the international scene, and her activities with the International Labour Organisation were noted in the tribute that appeared in the 1947 Annual Report.

Much comment is made in the Annual Reports about the expansion of international activities during the 1950s and 1960s, but the inspectors involved are very rarely named. It is therefore impossible to know how far women inspectors participated in these. We do know that Miss Cecily Tabb was the senior inspector chosen to go to Gibraltar in November 1973 at the request of the Overseas Development Administration. She spent a fortnight there preparing a report for the Deputy Governor of Gibraltar on *Factory inspection in Gibraltar*, where her brief had been to 'advise on the training of factory inspectors and on making the best possible use of the limited inspection resources.'

The Health and Safety at Work etc Act 1974

By 1974 industrial life, and factory inspection, had changed a great deal since the end of the Second World War. These changes meant that a new framework was needed for the conduct of inspection work. This was provided for in new legislation, which marked the end of an era for inspectors, and had been foreshadowed by the work of the committee under Lord Robens which had been appointed in 1970 by the Secretary of State for Employment, Mrs Barbara Castle. The committee was established to thoroughly review the provisions for the safety and health of people at work. Among those inspectors who liaised with this committee was Miss Beryl Leighton, then District Inspector in Huddersfield, who notes that she liaised 'with Professor Wood throughout the time the committee sat, taking him out to factories etc'. Miss Leighton retains a signed copy of the Report as a souvenir of this aspect of her work.

The committee presented its report in 1972, recommending the integration of all inspection work under a new authority, which in due course became the Health and Safety Executive (HSE). The Health and Safety at Work etc Act 1974 embodied the main recommendations of the Robens Report, widening the scope of health and safety legislation by abandoning the old definitions of premises and contracts of employment and extending protection to millions of people who had not previously been affected. Inspectors gained a new power, that of issuing improvement notices: and in cases of appeal, industrial tribunals, rather than the courts, were introduced.

Miss Audrey Pittom

Among the changes affecting women was the appointment of Miss Audrey Pittom, an inspector since 1945, and a Deputy Chief Inspector at this time, to be the first Director of the Hazardous Substances Group. This was one of the most senior appointments in the new HSE. She was subsequently appointed to serve on the Executive in 1977, until her retirement in 1978. She rose to the rank of Under-Secretary, thus becoming one of a small group of women who had become very senior civil servants, and the first woman to achieve this office within HSE.

Audrey Pittom's long career is recalled with admiration by those who worked with her. She was thorough, exceptionally hard-working, with a firm grasp of important issues, a tremendous memory, and the capacity to delegate, which is the mark of first class management.

Early in her career she became known as 'Seats Pittom', through her lectures and publications, including the widely used *Seating in industry* (probably the Department's first essay in the field of ergonomics). In the 1950s she worked with others to reduce power press accidents in the Midlands, and as Superintending Inspector in Nottingham gave:

    ❝informed and unswerving support to inspectors on the ground then trying to reduce siliceous dust and excessive heat both in the potteries and in the iron foundries of the area. " " (Hammer, unpublished)

Her work on lead, especially her skilful handling of the lead risks investigated by the Windeyer Committee in the 1970s, was widely recognised, and she was prominent in identifying and dealing with the newly discovered carcinogenity of vinyl chloride, a main constituent of many plastics. Here:

" " Miss Pittom's handling of the policy line of stringent controls, her chairing of the several committees of top industrialists and trade unions was outstanding. " " (Gates, unpublished)

Throughout her career Audrey Pittom argued forcefully for more attention to occupational health. As Jim Hammer recalls:

" " Typically it was Audrey who one day in early discussions on the proposed Safety and Health Bill said 'If we really want to give health a boost, it must come first in the title', and from that day on it became the Health and Safety at Work Bill - and so as an Act it has remained. " "

Miss Audrey Pittom

Women Specialist Inspectors

The history of specialist inspection in Britain is complicated by the existence of both separate specialist inspectorates, and of specialist inspectors within the Factory Department. The integration of these activities did not occur until the formation of the Health and Safety Executive in 1975. Historically, very few women have worked as specialist inspectors, so their contribution to these areas of work has inevitably been small. However, women did in the middle of the century gain a foothold in specialist inspection as Medical Inspectors and in one case as a Chemical Inspector, and in the past few years more women have begun to trickle into these areas of work.

The specialist inspectorates

The specialist inspectorates emerged in response to needs that were identified as industrialisation progressed, as industrial technology became more complex, and as humanitarian concerns about industrial welfare developed (see Table F). The Mines and Quarries Inspectorate came into being in the mid-nineteenth century: this is an area in which women have been unable to work because of legal prohibitions on female employment underground. In 1875 the Home

Table F. Women inspectors in the specialist inspectorates

Inspectorate	History	Current situation
Mines and Quarries	established 1843	0 women
Explosives	established 1875	12 men, 0 women
Railway	established 1840	0 women
Agriculture	established 1956	1985: 2 women/132 staff 1992: 15 women/185 staff
Nuclear Installations	established 1960	1985: 1 woman/102 staff 1992: 4 women/139 staff
Offshore	Division of HSE since 1991	1992: 3 woman/154 staff

(Derived from HSE statistics 1992)

Office established a small Explosives Inspectorate: again, no women have ever worked here. There were no women in railway inspector posts in 1992. Here historical disbarments on women's hours of employment mean that they have been unable to gain the relevant experience to enter this work through the traditional routes.

Under the Ministry of Agriculture, Fisheries and Food, specialist inspection was carried out by both safety inspectors and field officers by a staff which again was resolutely male for many years, but has recently included women, and it seems likely that women have now established a place in agricultural inspection work upon which they can build, although as yet, no women have been promoted to the grade of Principal Agriculture Inspector. The Nuclear Installations Inspectorate was established under the Nuclear Installations Act of 1959, and alongside it, following the Radioactive Substances Act 1960, a small inspectorate of radio-chemical inspectors was also formed. A few women are now nuclear inspectors within HSE, which may be the start of a more secure

place for women in nuclear inspection work.

Offshore safety work has achieved a high profile in recent years, especially after investigation into the Piper Alpha tragedy. This led to the establishment of a new Offshore Safety Division in HSE. Although initially with an all-male staff of inspectors, one woman, Sandra Caldwell, joined this Division as a Principal Inspector in 1991 working alongside 81 male colleagues.

Within the original Factory Department, specialist inspecting work developed in several different fields. These include medical inspection, and engineering, electrical, chemical and more latterly construction inspection. Only in medical and chemical inspection have women ever found a place, although in recent years a 'specialist inspector' designation has been established, and women occupied sixteen (approximately 7%) of these posts in April 1992. Table G shows the gradual increase in the number of specialist posts occupied by women between 1985 and 1992.

Medical inspection has perhaps been the most prominent of these fields, with the first medical inspector, Dr Thomas Legge, being appointed in 1898. In 1924 Miss S G Overton (born 1895) was appointed as H M Medical Inspector of Factories, the first woman to be so appointed; she later worked as Dr Sybil Horner, and reached the grade of Senior Medical Inspector of Factories in 1948, retiring in 1957. Ethel Browning, MD (also known as Mrs Ruston) was appointed to the established position of Medical Inspector in December 1948 (although Miss Curry thinks she was originally appointed on a temporary basis during the war). In 1953 women held three of the 14 posts in the medical inspector grades,

the third woman, Mrs J E Cottrell, having been appointed to work in Birmingham in 1947.

In chemical inspection, it was the appointment of Dr Marianne Woolgar to the Chemical Specialist Branch in 1957, which marked the significant step forward for women in the specialist areas. Dr Woolgar always hoped that she would not be the 'one and only' woman chemical inspector, but this was the case right up until her retirement in 1969. She trod a lonely path, with no-one following directly in her footsteps. By 1973, records still showed no woman in any of the specialist grades.

Table G. Women specialists in HSE 1985-1992 showing their share of specialist posts (women/all)

	Engineering	Construction	Chemical	Electrical	Specialist	All
1985	0/34	0/12	3/54	0/16	1/31	5/175
1986	0/35	0/13	3/54	0/19	1/40	5/184
1987	0/28	0/10	3/49	0/13	2/77	6/197
1988	0/24	0/11	3/45	0/14	2/86	6/197
1989	0/21	0/8	3/41	0/12	4/104	8/202
1990	0/18	0/8	2/36	0/12	7/120	10/207
1991	0/2	—	1/3	0/2	11/213	13/225
1992	—	—	—	—	16/243	16/245

Source: HSE Personnel Operations statistics, supplied July 1992

Dr Marianne Woolgar

Dr Woolgar rightly regarded it as a considerable achievement to attain her goal of becoming a chemical inspector, although it was one for which she was well qualified, having graduated from Birmingham University with First Class Honours (BSc) in Chemistry in 1931, and

subsequently been awarded a PhD in Chemistry by the same institution (1934).

Dr Woolgar entered the Factory Inspectorate during World War II, as noted above. After the war, she was appointed to an established position as H M Inspector of Factories, and worked in

Richmond, Surrey. She was promoted to Divisional Inspector in 1950, aged 41 years, and worked in the Factory Department's Southern Division, with Miss Schofield, 'a real Yorkshirewoman' whose abilities were admired by male and female staff alike, as her Superintending Inspector.

Dr Woolgar had already at the end of the 1940s and early in the 1950s been called upon to help train junior inspectors in aspects of their work for which her training as a chemist was especially useful, including taking them to factories where chemical regulations applied. These included factories where luminising work, which had greatly expanded during the war, was carried on. Inspectors knew, partly from American experience, what the dangers of luminising could be, and this work was carefully monitored. Regulations had been introduced in 1942 prohibiting the use of brushes for the application of luminous compounds to ensure that the deaths from cancer of the jaw, which American women workers had suffered after pointing their luminising brushes by mouth, could not be repeated.

This work brought Dr Woolgar into contact with the Senior Chemical Inspector, Mr S H Wilkes, and after a while he asked:

66 would I like to go and look after the Information Branch that was feeding (in) technical information? And I said, 'No. I want to come into the (Chemical) Branch', and he said, 'Well, if ever we have a woman in the Branch, it will be you'. 99

A little later, in 1957, a White Paper recommended that the Chemical Branch, along with some other parts of the Inspectorate, should be substantially expanded to meet the need for inspection of new products and new processes, many of which required chemical expertise.

66 It was trawled within the Department for people with scientific qualifications to apply for vacancies in the Chemical Branch. And there were two men that applied with me. Well, we all went in together, but they kept me (based) in the District, and I didn't get into the Headquarters for three weeks. But one of the women inspectors, a senior one, went and saw Mr Wilkes, and said 'Look, you've got to have her up here'. ... I'd heard whispers, you know - no woman, over my dead body - but I thought, it's up to me, I'm not going to make any sort of point about this - it's the JOB I want to do.

I think they thought, if they had a woman, they'd have to carry the instruments. So I made a point. I said 'I'll bring the instruments!' (laughs). And we'd meet on the station. 'Give 'em here!', they'd say! We had meetings, once a month, to discuss things, and the Senior Inspector said, 'Come on chaps! - and that means YOU!' And I thought, Ooh, I've been accepted now. But I must say they were all perfect gentlemen . 99

Her work now brought her into close contact with the Radiological Protection Laboratory at Teddington, as efforts to enforce the luminising regulations and other chemical regulations were strictly enforced. In such factories, she recalls:

66 all the stocks had to be kept in a cabinet under mechanical exhaust extraction, at least, before you opened the door, so that any radon (which was one of the decay products of radium) was taken out of the workroom. You could find cabinets where people worked and did the application in an enclosed cabinet, and this only improved over the years, because there was much too much access. You'd to be very careful about the efficient flow of air through. 99

Jane Bugler, specialist inspector in process safety

After a while, Dr Woolgar was sent to the Atomic Energy Research Establishment at Harwell, to undertake further training for her radiological protection work. Her certificate, issued by the UK Atomic Energy Authority on completion of the course at the Isotope School, refers to her as 'He', suggesting how very much she was still a pioneer as a woman working in this field.

As she became more experienced in this specialist work, Dr Woolgar was called upon to share her expertise. She gave various lectures, including some to the Women's Engineering Association about ionising radiation, and later, with one of her colleagues, John Rees, became involved in work promoting health and safety in research establishments. This was done through the Information and Advisory unit to implement the Code of Practice on Ionising Radiations produced by the Radioactive Substances Advisory Committee chaired by Professor Sir Brian Windeyer.

This work took her all over the country, to universities, medical schools, research councils, and private industry. She went frequently to Edinburgh where 'there were 42 departments using radioactive materials', and especially enjoyed her visits to

Kathlyn Heywood, specialist inspector in biosafety

Birmingham. This was the period when universities, she recalls, began appointing safety officers:

66 They used to ring up and ask about health and safety matters, and I was only too glad to help. I found that the universities ... don't like nit-picking, but they were very practical, and if you had positive advice to give them, they took it. 99 (interview with Marianne Woolgar 1992)

In 1967 she and John Rees published an article entitled *Radiological protection in research and teaching*, which appeared in the Ministry of Labour Gazette, and explained the work which they had been

doing in this field, giving examples of the kinds of hazard that could arise and what steps could be taken to avoid them.

Her work was greatly helped, Dr Woolgar recalls, by her membership of the Radiation Research Association. This was an international body, and in about 1960 its activities took her on a particularly interesting foreign trip. The meeting:

66 started with three days in Karlsruhe where we visited the 'Kernreaktor', the German equivalent of the Atomic Energy Research Establishment at Harwell, and was then followed by three days of meetings at CERN, the European Research

Janet Etchells, principal specialist inspector

Establishment, just outside Geneva. These included tours of laboratories and delivery of papers on original research work into various aspects of investigations of exposure to ionising radiations. Such information helped to provide a wider understanding of the risks involved. 99

Dr Woolgar retired at the age of 60 in 1969, when she had been the only woman chemical inspector for 12 years. Now in her mid-eighties, living near to her childhood home, where the monument to 17 children killed in a factory fire in 1815 had so impressed her as a child, she remains very active, and maintains contacts with past colleagues. Her interview and other contributions, on which this account is based, are suggestive of the intelligence and enthusiasm which must have marked her out for her seniors in the postwar years. She is also striking for her good humour and sense of fun. This came over clearly in her recollections of the difficulties when working in the general staff and prior to her transfer to Chemical Branch - which in her estimation were surprisingly few - of working as a lone woman in a specialised area dominated by men. Once, when out inspecting in a factory, she overheard the occupier comment: 'It's a woman,' as she arrived.

Women specialist inspectors in 1992

The women working in the field of specialist inspection in 1992 include a number of women in their 30s who have entered the profession with degrees in science and engineering, and some other industrial or safety experience. Details of a few of them can indicate the kind of work they do and the varied backgrounds from which they come.

Janet Etchells graduated from Birmingham University with a degree in chemical engineering in 1975. After five years working in industry and the MOD she joined HSE in 1980, and has specialised in fire and explosion hazards, working with industries as diverse as milk powder spray drying, micro-chip manufacture, oil refineries, explosives production, power stations, breweries and scrapyards. Since her promotion to Principal Specialist Inspector her work has included fire and explosion hazards associated with exothermic reaction processes and the storing and handling of highly reactive and energetic materials. Perhaps in her Dr Woolgar has found an appropriate successor.

Jane Bugler is a more recent recruit to HSE, joining in 1988 as a specialist inspector in process safety with a background including a degree in chemical engineering and eight years' industrial experience. Like Janet Etchells, her work has included assessing the standards for storing, handling and using hazardous substances. She has also been involved in accident investigations and associated legal work.

From a rather different background, in environmental health, Pritti Shah now works in the Manchester area as a specialist inspector in occupational hygiene, giving technical advice and expert opinion on a wide variety of occupational hygiene matters, and collects monitoring data through technical survey work.

Susan Forster, another 'descendant' of Marianne Woolgar perhaps, works as a specialist inspector of radiological protection. She has a degree in biochemistry from the University of Keele, and a background in biochemical research. She now gives specialist advice on radiological protection in a range of contexts including nuclear medicine in hospitals, particle accelerators in universities, and site radiography.

Pritti Shah, specialist inspector in occupational hygiene

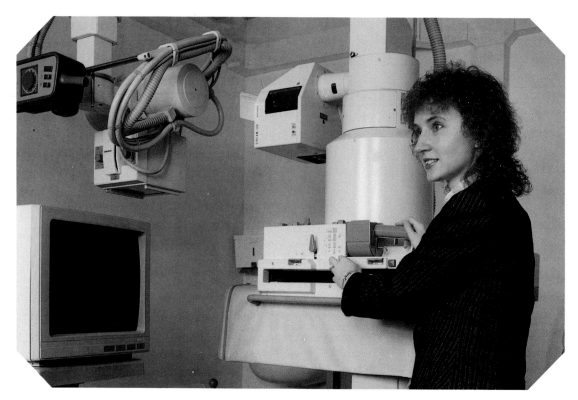

Susan Forster, specialist inspector of radiological protection

As a specialist inspector in biosafety, Kathlyn Heywood inspects sites handling dangerous pathogens, including research establishments, isolation hospitals and laboratories. She entered HSE in 1985 with a background in the National Health Service, having obtained degree level qualifications on a part-time basis while with the NHS.

The women currently working in specialist inspection are, as Table G shows, still in a small minority in their area of work. Nevertheless the expansion of inspection work in this field in recent years, and the growth of opportunities in higher education with women gradually increasing their participation in degree courses in science and engineering, offers hope that this small group of women will continue to expand, and to gain access to the more senior positions in this field in the future.

The experience of women inspectors today

One hundred years after the appointment of the first women inspectors of factories, how secure is the position of women within the profession, and what is the contemporary role of the woman inspector?

Women's representation in factory inspecting

There are today approximately 175 women in the grades of factory inspector, and almost one quarter of all factory inspectors are female. Although this does not reach the target figure of 30% set, but never achieved, in the interwar period, there has been considerable recent improvement on a situation which after World War II seemed for a while to be deteriorating.

The figures in Table G show that there has been considerable recent improvement, although women remain disproportionately few at the top. The marked increase in the numbers of women in the more junior factory inspector grades in part reflects an active equal opportunities policy where recruitment has been specially targeted.

Equality of opportunity for women, on the

agenda of senior women inspectors like Hilda Martindale so many years before, gathered momentum in the years after the formation of the Health and Safety Executive in 1975. The passage of the Sex Discrimination Act in 1975, and pressure for action on equal opportunities issues from various groups within the Civil Service led to a Programme of Action to Achieve Equality of Opportunity for Women in 1984.

This policy has been actively pursued within HSE, and today the organisation has a five-year Equal Opportunities Action Programme to increase the representation of women and other previously disadvantaged groups. Tangible results of this programme can be seen in the figures in Table H and

in developments such as the workplace nursery at the Bootle office, and holiday playschemes in various part of the country. Four members of staff have become designated 'harassment advisers', trained to give confidential advice and counselling to staff who feel they are the subject of harassment, including sexual harassment, at work. A Career Break scheme has been established, enabling staff to take up to five years' unpaid leave with no loss of seniority, and this is supported by 'keeping-in-touch' and 'work experience' arrangements. In this way, HSE now seeks to enable women and men 'to combine a satisfying career with domestic and other responsibilities'.

Table II. Women factory inspectors in selected grades 1985-92

Women as a % of all inspectors in grade with actual numbers in brackets

	1985	1986	1987	1988	1989	1990	1991	1992
DCIF	0 (0)	0 (0)	0 (0)	0 (0)	0 (0)	0 (0)	0 (0)	0 (0)
SIF	0 (0)	8 (1)	6 (1)	6 (1)	10 (2)	13 (3)	17 (4)	26 (6)
DSIF	15 (5)	11 (4)	14 (5)	14 (5)	12 (4)	10 (3)	10 (3)	7 (2)
Insp 1A	3 (4)	4 (5)	5 (7)	5 (7)	5 (8)	6 (9)	6 (10)	7(12)
Insp 1B	18 (47)	18(47)	18(44)	20(54)	22(60)	23(68)	25(72)	25(72)
Insp 2	34(14)	31(16)	30(24)	30(21)	30(30)	35(46)	39(62)	42(84)
All grades	14(70)	14(73)	15(81)	16(88)	17(104)	20(129)	22(151)	24(176)

Key:

DCIF -   Deputy Chief Inspector of Factories
SIF   -   Superintending Inspector of Factories
DSIF -   Deputy Superintending Inspector of Factories

Source: Derived from HSE Personnel Operations statistics

Women Factory Inspectors and their work today

The figures given in Table H suggest ways in which HSE has recently made efforts to give women equality of opportunity in the career of factory inspector. To see what women working as inspectors themselves felt about their careers, a small number of current inspectors were asked to supply personal information relating to their own experience, and to comment upon the position of women in factory inspection. The women who gave this information ranged from recent recruits in the most junior grades to Area Director.

Background and experience

Like their much earlier predecessors, women factory inspectors today come from diverse educational backgrounds. Some are university educated women with degrees in scientific subjects (eg botany, zoology, applied biology), while others have graduated in arts and the humanities (eg politics and history, French and Italian, human communication). Others obtained their qualifications through part-time study (eg Linda Williams, now Area Director in South Yorkshire and Humberside, becoming a Licentiate and Associate of the Institute of Metallurgists, and later gaining a Masters degree in metallurgy and materials technology following earlier day release study to obtain an HNC in metallurgy). Caroline Wake joined HSE relatively recently having become a licentiate of the Royal Society of Chemistry.

Some women inspectors have entered inspection work at the beginning of their careers, while others have considerable work experience on joining HSE. Previous jobs include posts as technicians, technologists, laboratory supervisors, operatives, supervisors and managers.

Recruitment and training

All those who gave personal information spoke favourably about their training as factory inspectors. The diploma course at the University of Aston (leading to a qualification in occupational safety and hygiene) had been the centrepiece of the training for many, and had provided for some an important introduction into the culture of factory inspection work and an opportunity to make contact with other new recruits. On-the-job training, which was enjoyed and much praised, gave access to contact with older inspectors, whose advice and encouragement was regarded as invaluable. Those who had been trained by senior women inspectors found their advice particularly helpful.

Factory inspection as a career for women

As might be expected, all the women who supplied information felt inspection was an appropriate job for women. Indeed, some believed there were distinct advantages in being a woman, especially in contacts with occupiers. However, there was recognition that women may face special obstacles in their careers (including discrimination).

The status and powers of factory inspectors were regarded as important factors enabling women to carry out their work of inspection relatively freely. Although some had met with amusement and surprise on account of their sex (an experience also mentioned by the retired women inspectors), such responses from employers were readily overcome by a practical, businesslike approach, and by the fact that:

> 66 most seem aware of your powers as an inspector, and treat you accordingly. 99

Several women admitted that the job could at times be dangerous or frightening ('although it could be the same for a man'), but believed that being female offered them some protection from assault.

> 66 I can think of at least two incidents where my sex probably saved me from being physically assaulted.
> I have NEVER been refused entry to a premises. I know many of my colleagues have, and the ones I know about were men. 99

Another commented that she had 'never needed to take a male colleague for support or protection'.

Some of the women felt it was easier for women to defuse potentially violent or aggressive confrontations. One commented 'men accept criticism more easily from a woman', and another:

> 66 I particularly recommend being pregnant and inspecting. Aggressive and hostile occupiers can't quite keep up the game-cock stance. 99

Although one junior woman felt that her personal lack of technical qualifications was a disadvantage when inspecting, others felt that their relative ease in admitting ignorance was at times beneficial:

> 66 I trained under a female District Inspector who was well respected by local industry. She taught me to say 'I don't know' if I didn't. I think this is something men find very difficult. I found the wire drawers of Warrington were only too happy to tell me about the mysteries of wortle plates when I confessed my total ignorance. 99

Within their own organisation, women had noticed changes in attitudes to women inspectors over the years. Although sometimes feeling as if they were 'on trial for all womankind', most had mainly positive experiences, and emphasised that male colleagues were generally friendly and supportive. Those who had been inspectors before the formation of HSE in 1975 felt that some of the more 'chauvinist' attitudes had gradually drained away. One quite senior woman remarked:

> 66 Six years ago I was told by my (male) Area Director that I could not inspect shipbuilding, heavy engineering or construction activities. I am therefore all the more delighted to be leading a group of inspectors responsible for ... construction and demolition activities. 99

Those who had children explained how they had succeeded in combining their careers with family responsibilities. Several had taken maternity leave, returning either to full or part-time work, while older women were more likely to have taken a longer (unofficial) career break. One commented that, returning in the 1970s, she was at first offered only one-year contracts, and that 'it was with some difficulty that I became re-established'. No concessions were made, and she felt she was 'closely monitored to check I was not taking time off to see to the children'.

Managing a demanding job and a young family was difficult - 'I needed a wife'; 'I wouldn't ever do it again' - but childminders, au pairs, supportive husbands, partners and families had made it possible. Although family responsibilities could be a constraint - for example, affecting geographical mobility and ability to commute long distances - several women pointed out that men in their 30s and 40s often faced similar difficulties. It had been possible to 'turn in a good job', to gain promotion, and even to accept short-term assignments abroad.

Range of women inspectors' work

Today, women appear to have gained access to almost all areas of factory inspection work. Although inspection in industries such as shipbuilding and construction was regarded as inappropriate for women until relatively recently, sex discrimination legislation, the gradual erosion of sexist attitudes, and women's own determination and ability have combined to create a much less discriminatory environment.

Even among the small group of women who supplied information about their own careers there was a wide range of experience of factory inspection work. They had inspected foundries and motor manufacturing, general engineering, textiles, food, drink and printing, plastics, footwear, construction, health services, fairgrounds, and education. Among their specialisms they included microbiological hazards, woodworking, leather, and robotics and programmable electronic systems.

Some had been involved in policy development work, for example in the consultation process associated with the development of proposals regarding the Control of Substances Hazardous to Health Regulations, and as secretary to the Equal Opportunities Commission working party investigating discriminatory aspects of health and safety legislation. The latter brought into recent focus themes which had concerned women factory inspectors since the 1890s: women's hours of employment, lead regulation, lifting and pregnancy.

Others, again like some of their much earlier predecessors, had travelled abroad on inspection business, in one case studying the training of factory inspectors in France, and in another attending meetings of the ILO and the World Health Organisation in France and Geneva as an HSE leather specialist.

The legacy of the past

Women's contribution to the promotion of health and safety in employment through one hundred years of work in factory inspection has been remarkable. In the early decades that work was accomplished by a small group of dedicated, determined and energetic women, motivated above all by their compassionate concern for the welfare of women workers and their families, whose harsh conditions of life and labour they had seen for themselves and were determined to improve.

In wartime, women took on a wider role in factory inspection, becoming acquainted with the men's trades, into which women workers had been newly introduced, and finding that no area of inspection work need be closed to them. As the century progressed there were setbacks, but the uneven progress of women's emancipation in society was reflected in developments within the Factory Inspectorate.

The incorporation of the women's branch into the men's inspectorate was controversial and not without its disadvantages, although ultimately it can be judged to have been beneficial. In the full employment years of the 1950s and 1960s, when there was general difficulty in recruiting factory inspectors, women inspectors became much less numerous, and lost their reserved place in the senior ranks. During those years, when there were fewer capable and enthusiastic young women entering the profession, it fell to an earlier generation of inspectors, particularly those who had been recruited in the 1930s and during World War II to work steadily, and in many cases with some distinction, to maintain the standards of work which their predecessors had set.

After the establishment of HSE in 1975 women inspectors, although now relatively small in number, became beneficiaries of wider improvements in the social status of women. Protected now by legislation, they could claim equality of opportunity with enhanced authority, and during the last decade with the active assistance of their own organisation.

Prospects for the future

Recent progress towards 25% of factory inspectors being female has been achieved largely through recruitment of women into junior ranks. At the close of the twentieth century, it seems likely that fewer women inspectors will quit the profession on marriage or motherhood than has previously been the case, while recent promotions of women to senior positions suggest that capable and committed women are making their way into senior grades without being unduly handicapped by their domestic responsibilities. Both these factors indicate that women now have a secure and still growing place within the work of factory inspection.

The testimony of current inspectors indicates that factory inspection is a profession combining technical, scientific, legal and humanitarian concerns. Women inspectors find their work challenging, stimulating and demanding, and mostly feel that they have the support of their colleagues (male and female) and of their management. The environment in which women inspectors work has changed almost beyond recognition since 1893, yet there remains a feeling that women do indeed have something special to offer. As one junior inspector put it in 1992:

" I hope women will be able to evolve their own techniques of inspection and not rely on or feel compelled to try and emulate traditional male approaches as if they were a preferable norm which must be achieved. "

Women factory inspectors have through the years acknowledged the support and assistance which many of their male colleagues have given. It in no way denigrates men's achievements in this role to say, after one hundred years of women factory inspectors, that women's fine record of achievement and commitment to the cause of health and safety in the workplace is one of which they can be justly proud.

Bibliography

Books and other published material

Anderson, A M (1922) *Women in the factory: an administrative adventure* John Murray, London

(ARCI) *Annual Reports of the Chief Inspector of Factories and Workshops 1802-1974* HMSO

Blackburn, E K (1985) *When I grew up* Brookside Press, Accrington, Lancs

Boston, S (1980) *Women workers and the trade unions* Davis Poynter, London

Harrison, B (1989) Some of them gets poisoned: occupational lead exposure in women, 1880-1914 *Social History of Medicine* Vol 2 No 2 August

Harrison, B (1990) Suffer the working day: women in the 'dangerous trades,' 1880-1914 *Women's Studies International Forum* Vol 13 Nos 1/2 Pergamon Press

Health and Safety Executive (1980) *A brief history of HM Factory Inspectorate* (out of print)

Health and Safety Executive (1990) *Health and safety: a challenge for specialists* HSE, Bootle

Health and Safety Executive (1991) *A career with the Health and Safety Executive* Offshore Safety Division HSE, Bootle

Holcombe, L (1973) *Victorian ladies at work: middle class working women in England and Wales 1850-1914* David and Charles, Newton Abbott, published in 1974 by Shoe String Publishers, ISBN 0 208 01340 7

Home Office (1930) *Report of Departmental Committee of Factory Inspectors* (out of print)

Home Office *Minutes of evidence taken before the inter-departmental Committee on Physical Deterioration* 3 volumes: CD 2175, CD 2210, CD 2186 (out of print)

Hutchins, B L & Harrison, A (1966) *A history of factory legislation* 3rd edition Frank Cass & Co London

Ilford Recorder (1947) edition of 2 October

Jones, H (1988) Women health workers: the case of the first women factory inspectors in Britain *Social History of Medicine* Vol 1 No 2 August

McFeely, M D (1988) *Lady inspectors: the campaign for a better workplace 1893-1921* Basil Blackwell, New York

Martindale, H (1938) *Women servants of the state 1870-1938: a history of women in the civil service* George Allen and Unwin, London

Martindale, H (1944) *From one generation to another 1839-1944* George Allen and Unwin, London

Messiter, F E (1950) A study of the Operations at Unfenced Machinery Regulations *Safety Equipment and Industrial Clothing* 2nd edition (out of print)

Squire, R E (1927) *Thirty years in the public service: an industrial retrospect* Nisbet and Co, London

Tabb, C V & Malins Smith, K [eds] (1985) *Recollections of some former inspectors of factories* Private printing

Wilson, J (1983) *Women factory inspectors*

Woolgar, M D & Rees, J M (1967) Radiological protection in research and teaching *Ministry of Labour Gazette*

Unpublished sources

Curry, N (1955) Opening statement for the prosecution, handwritten

Factory Department Staff Lists 1954 and 1973

Factory Department (1955) Enforcement Notice, issued 19 May.

Health and Safety Executive Personnel Operations Statistics 1985-1992

Letters, K Crundwell to N Curry December 1961

Letter, M D Woolgar to S M Yeandle 8 May 1992

Printed in the UK for HSE, published by HMSO

C40   1.93

130